ISBN 978-1-330-00601-6
PIBN 10002054

1 MONTH OF
FREE
READING

at

www.ForgottenBooks.com

By purchasing this book you are eligible for one month membership to ForgottenBooks.com, giving you unlimited access to our entire collection of over 700,000 titles via our web site and mobile apps.

To claim your free month visit: www.forgottenbooks.com/free2054

Similar Books Are Available from
www.forgottenbooks.com

ANCIENT HISTORY.

CONTENTS.

————▸◄◂————

INTRODUCTION, ... 4

CHAPTER I.

EGYPT.

Section 1. Ancient Empire: First Dynasties of
Memphis and the building of the Pyramids.
Middle Empire: First Dynasties of Thebes and
Invasion of the Hyksos, or Shepherd-kings, . 11

Section 2. New Empire: Conquests and Monuments of the Kings of the eighteenth and nineteenth Dynasties, Thoutmosis III. and Ramses
II., or Sesostris, ... 20

Section 3. Decline of the New Empire: The Ethiopian Kings (725–665 B.C.) and the Saïte Kings
(665–525 B.C.)—Conquest of Egypt by Cambyses (525 B.C.)—Institutions, Religion, and
Manners of the Egyptians, . . 27

CHAPTER II.

ASSYRIA AND BABYLONIA.

Section 1. Babylon and Ninive: First Assyrian Em-
pire (1314–789 B.C.)—Salmanasar IV. (905–871
B.C.)—Second Assyrian Empire (744–625 B.C.)—
Sennacherib (704–681 B.C.), ... 45

3

CONTENTS.

———✠———

Section 2. Babylonian or Chaldean Empire (625–588 B.C.) : Nabuchodonosor the Great (604–561 B.C.)—Taking of Babylon by Cyrus (538 B.C.) —Institutions, Religion, and Manners of the Assyrians and Babylonians, ...   57

Section 3. Religion, Government, etc.,.   .   65

CHAPTER III.

MEDIA AND PERSIA.

Section 1. Origin of the Medes and Persians.—Government of the Medes before Cyrus (650–559 B.C.)—Conquest and Empire of Cyrus (559–529 B.C.), ...   70

Section 2. Cambyses (529–522 B.C.)—The False Smerdis (522–521 B.C.)—Darius I. before the Median Wars (521–500 B.C.)—Institutions, Religion, and Manners of the Medes and Persians,   80

CHAPTER IV.

PHŒNICIA AND CARTHAGE.

Section 1. Sidon and Tyre.—Commerce, Colonies, Industry, and Religion of the Phœnicians,   91

Section 2. Carthage : her Conquests.—War in Sicily (fifth and fourth centuries).—Manners and Institutions of the Carthaginians,   .   .   .   95

CHAPTER V.

GREECE.

Section 1. Primitive Times.—Sparta : Laws of Lycurgus.—Messenian Wars.—Athens : Laws of Solon.—Pisistratus and his Sons (561–510 B.C.) —Institutions, Religion, and Manners of Ancient Greece, ...   105

—✦—

Section 2. Median Wars (500–449 B.C.)—First War:
Battle of Marathon (490 B.C.)—Second War:
Battles of Salamis (480 B.C.), Platæa, and Mycale (479 B.C.)—Third War: Victories of Cimon; Treaty of Peace (449 B.C.), . . 128

Section 3. Peloponnesian War (431–404 B.C)—Pre-
ponderance of Athens.—Pericles.—Alcibiades.
—Taking of Athens (404 B.C.)—Retreat of the
Ten Thousand (401–400 B.C.)—Socrates.—Pre-
ponderance of Sparta.—Rivalry of Athens and
Sparta, ... 140

CHAPTER VI.

MACEDONIA.—EMPIRE OF ALEXANDER THE GREAT.

Section 1. Philip (360–337 B.C.)—First Sacred War
(355–345 B.C.)—Second Sacred War.—Battle of
Chæronea (338 B.C.), ... 165

Section 2. Alexander the Great (336–323 B.C.)—
Submission of Greece.—Conquests in Asia.
Ruin of the Persian Empire, ... 171

Section 3. Dismemberment of the Empire of Alexander the Great — Anarchy of twenty-two
years (323–301 B.C.)—Antigonus and Demetrius.—Battle of Ipsus (301 B.C.), . . . 183

CHAPTER VII.

STATES FORMED FROM THE DISMEMBERMENT OF ALEXANDER'S EMPIRE.

Section 1. Egypt under the Lagi (323–30 B.C.)—Its
Glory and Prosperity under the first three Pto-
lemies (323–222 B.C.) Rivalry with Syria.—
Anarchy and the Intervention of the Romans, 190

6 CONTENTS.

---+---

Section 2. The Kingdom of Syria under the Seleucidæ (301–64 B.C.)—Power of Seleucus I.—Antiochus the Great (222–186 B C.)—Intervention of the Romans, ... 198

Section 3. Kingdom of Macedonia (319–148 B.C.) and Greece (301–146 B.C.)—Triumph of the Family of Antigonus in Macedonia.—Anarchy in Greece.—Reforms at Sparta.—Intervention of the Romans.—Kings Philip (221–178 B.C.) and Perseus (178–168 B C.)—The Achæan League : Aratus and Philopœmen, . 206

Chronological Table of Ancient History, . 229

INTRODUCTION.

THE advent of the Messias, which is the crowning event of history, divides it into two parts: *Ancient History*, or that time which preceded the birth of Jesus Christ, and *Modern History*, or the time which has elapsed since that event. This division is so natural that, by referring all events to Jesus Christ, we give to history its unity: in ancient times by *Sacred History*, or that of the people chosen to prepare the way for the advent of the Messias, and in modern times by the *History of the Church*, or that of the society set up to propagate throughout the world the work of the Saviour.

Prevailing usage, however, divides universal history into three parts: *Ancient History*, from the creation to the division of the Roman Empire, in 395; *Mediæval History*, from the said division to the taking of Constantinople by the Ottoman Turks, in 1453; *Modern History*, from the taking of Constantinople to contemporary events.

Under *Ancient History* is commonly included *Sacred History*, or that of the people of God, from the Creation to the birth of Jesus Christ in the reign of Herod, King of Judea; *Oriental History*—*i.e.*, of the Egyptians, Assyrians and Babylonians, Medes and Persians, Phœnicians and Carthaginians; *Grecian History*, from the remotest times to the conquest by the Romans; finally, *Roman History*, from the foundation of Rome to the division of the Roman Empire at the death of Theodosius the Great, in 395.

Ancient History comprises the history of the Oriental and Grecian nations only; but it is connected with sacred history either at its starting-point, which is the dispersion of men after the Deluge, or because the Oriental and Grecian nations became more or less connected with the people of God. Thus, that people find in Egypt their cradle and early trials. After their settlement in the promised land other nations become to them instruments of justice or of mercy: God makes use of the Phœnicians to aid them to build the Temple; of the Assyrians and Babylonians to chastise them; of the Persians to reinstate them; of Alexander and his first successors to protect them; of the kings of Syria to try them by persecution; and, finally, of the Romans to maintain them against the kings of Syria, who seek their destruction.

Ancient History is divided into seven parts, according to the succession of empires:

I. Egypt from remotest times to the conquest of Cambyses, King of the Persians, B.C. 525.

II. Assyria and Babylon, from the foundation of Babylon and Ninive to the taking of Babylon by Cyrus, B.C. 538.

III. Media and Persia, from the origin of these states to the beginning of the Median wars, B.C. 500.

IV. Phœnicia and Carthage, from the origin of the Phœnicians to the beginning of the Punic wars, B.C. 264.

V. Greece, from the origin of the Greeks to the accession of Philip, King of Macedonia, B.C. 360.

VI. Macedonia and the empire of Alexander the Great, from the accession of Philip to the battle of Ipsus, or the partition of the empire of Alexander the Great, B.C. 301.

VII. The states formed from the dismemberment of the empire of Alexander the Great, from the battle of Ipsus to the conquest by the Romans.

To render this edition more complete and exact we have endeavored to profit by the important discoveries of our age. Without entering into a discussion which would here be out of place, we shall limit ourselves to two observations: first, that we have admitted none but certain facts, and in a few instances only, in default of certainty, most probable opinions; second, that when the results of the researches of the learned attain certainty, they are always found in accordance with the Bible. Thus, it was at first asserted that the original inhabitants

—✠—

of Egypt came from Ethiopia, and had peopled the country by descending the valley of the Nile; at present it is accepted as an indubitable fact that they came from the East, conformably to the account in Genesis, and that they peopled Egypt by ascending the valley of the Nile. A similar error occurred in regard to the famous zodiac of Denderah: chronologists mistakenly proclaimed it anterior to the Deluge of Genesis; but more competent critics now declare it to be posterior to the beginning of the Christian era. Science worthy of the name can but aid the triumph of truth.

ANCIENT HISTORY.

CHAPTER I.

EGYPT.

THE history of Egypt, from the remotest times to the domination of the Persians, comprises twenty-six dynasties, and is divided into three periods: 1. The *Ancient Empire*, signalized by the building of the Pyramids, and the *Middle Empire*, destroyed by the invasion of the Hyksos, or shepherd-kings. 2. The *New Empire*, founded by the kings of the eighteenth and nineteenth dynasties. 3. The decline of the New Empire, from the end of the fourteenth century B.C. to the conquest of Egypt by Cambyses, King of the Persians, B.C. 525.

We follow the division adopted by the learned, without admitting as successive all the dynasties enumerated by Manetho, an Egyptian historian of the third century B.C. A certain number of dynasties reigned simultaneously, and there are several known to us only by the names of their kings. Egyptian chronology, very obscure till the year 1300 B.C., offers a succession of certain dates only since the seventh century B.C.

Sec. 1. **ANCIENT EMPIRE**: *First Dynasties of Memphis and the building of the Pyramids.*
Middle Empire: *First Dynasties of Thebes and the Invasion of the Hyksos, or Shepherd-kings.*

FOUNDATION OF MEMPHIS IN THE VALLEY OF THE NILE.—After the dispersion of men, Mis-

11

raïm, son of Cham, peopled Egypt, called from
his name the land of Misraim.   Menes, however,
one of his descendants, must be regarded as the
true founder of the monarchy.   To check the
waters of the Nile, which spread westward towards the sands of Libya, he dug a new bed for
the river, and built upon the left bank a city
which he called Memphis, or "the good residence."   Thus this prince had the glory of giving to Egypt its first capital, and of commencing
the works of irrigation which have since rendered
the Nile the source of the riches and beauty of
the country.

As it seldom rains in Egypt, the Nile by its
annual inundation supplies that defect.   It is
no longer a matter of dispute that this inundation is owing to the rains that fall in Nubia and
Abyssinia, from whence this river flows, bearing
along in its course a rich alluvium.   The inundation begins with summer, and increases till
the first days of autumn.   As soon as the waters
subside seed is sown, and the time of harvest is
in March.   Egypt presents two widely differ-
ing spectacles at two seasons of the year.   In
August it is a vast sea, in which appear towns
and villages, with causeways leading from place
to place, the whole interspersed with groves and
fruit-trees, whose tops only are visible.   In Janu-
ary the whole country is one continued scene of
beautiful meadows enamelled with flowers; the

air is perfumed by the blossoms of the orange, lemon, and other trees; so that nature, being dead, as it were, in other climes, seems to put on added bloom in the Nile valley.

THE PYRAMIDS.—The successors of Menes, reigning at Memphis over a country at once rich and populous, soon extended their sway from the Libyan deserts to Mount Sínai. We may judge of their power by the construction of the famous pyramids, which have triumphed over time and the inroads of barbarians. The largest of the three is attributed to Cheops, a king of the fourth dynasty. It forms a perfect square, each side of which measures 669 feet at the base. Its perpendicular height is 462 feet; and its summit, which from below seems a point, is a platform measuring 15 feet on each side. During a period of thirty years one hundred thousand men, succeeding each other in relays every three months, were constantly employed upon this work. It is worthy of remark that the four sides of the pyramid are turned exactly to the four cardinal points, and show the true meridian of the place. The structure also testifies to the skill of the Egyptian architects, by preserving uninjured under its weight after so many ages the galleries and halls leading to the centre or king's chamber. "But what efforts soever men may make, their nothingness," says Bossuet, "will always appear." The great pyramid was a tomb, but the chamber of the king remained empty; Cheops became so odious to his subjects that he was not suffered to be buried therein. His brother Chéphrèn, who built the second pyramid, was also denied sepulchre there. Their successors, nevertheless, followed their example, and more than sixty pyramids yet standing attest the vain ambition of the Egyptian kings to have their mortal remains repose in immortal monuments.*

LAKE MŒRIS.—A work of greater utility than the pyramids, and not less famous in antiquity, was Lake Mœris, so called from the name of a king of the sixth dynasty. The overflowing of the Nile rendered Egypt fertile only inasmuch as it attained a certain height, too great or too little rise of the waters being equally fatal to the country. To correct this irregularity, King Mœris caused a very deep lake to be dug about ten leagues in circumference. This served as a vast reservoir, which received the waters of the river when they rose too high, and replenished them when they fell too low. Not to lose too much

* King Mycerinus, also belonging to the fourth dynasty, undertook the erection of the third great pyramid. In it was found his coffin, which is now in the British Museum. The three great pyramids of Gizeh, a village between Cairo and Memphis, deserved to be reckoned among the Seven Wonders of the world. The other reputed wonders of the ancient world were: the pharos (or watchtower) of Alexandria, in Lower Egypt; the colossus of Rhodes; the tomb of Mausolus, King of Caria; the temple of Diana at Ephesus; the statue of Jupiter Olympus, by Phidias; and the labyrinth of Crete, attributed to Dædalus.

—✦—

arable land in the construction of the lake, it was extended principally on the Libyan side. The fisheries brought in considerable revenue; and therefore when the land produced nothing they drew from it treasures by covering it with water. From the centre of the lake two massive columns, upholding on two thrones colossal statues of Mœris and his consort, rose three hundred feet above its surface and sank a great distance below. On the shores of the lake were built palaces and pleasure-houses; so that this work, so useful to Egypt, became also a delightful resort for the inhabitants of Memphis.

CLOSING SPLENDORS AND END OF THE ANCIENT EMPIRE.—King Mœris, whose power many inscriptions attest, established trade with Asia by the Red Sea, and carried his victorious arms as far as Ethiopia. His reign seems to have cast a radiance over the ancient Egyptian empire, which is scarcely known to us except by its subterranean tombs. All the scenes of aristocratic life in those remote times are there depicted: the functions of dignitaries at court; their diverse, occupations in the country—some engaged in hunting on their vas' domains, others fishing in sail-boats on the Nile and the neighboring canals; all surrounded with a crowd of servants who till their farms and raise immense flocks. A fact worthy of note in this patriarchal life is longevity. A king of the sixth dynasty, supposed to be Mœris himself, occupied the throne a hundred years ; and a little before a royal personage, having attained the age of a hundred and ten years, put to profit his long experience by giving his son precepts of morality that have come down to us.*

But the most ancient empire of the world was to perish, like so many others, in the frenzy of civil war. Ambition, the vice inseparable from riches and greatness, raised up competitors to the kings of the sixth dynasty. The last of these occupied the throne but a year, when he was slain by an assassin. His sister, Nïtocris, not less famous for wisdom than for beauty, seized the reins of government, and for twelve years caused the custom to be blessed that granted women the right to govern Egypt. A queen so dear to her subjects easily completed the construction of the third great pyramid, in which she hoped to be buried; but she did not renounce a project of signal vengeance on her brother's murderers. All the accomplices, allured by fine promises into a subterranean hall, were giving themselves

---

* This veteran, named Phtah-Hoten—i.e., *Phtah*, or the *peaceful Sun*—especially reminds his son what he owes to God and to his mother : " It is God who gave life to thy mother and to thee. Thy mother, having brought thee into the world, clasped thee to her bosom and fed thee with her milk three years. She lavished upon thee unwearied care. When I said, ' Come, it is time to put him to school,' and when thou wast learning to write, she went every day to thy master's house to bring thee something to eat and to drink. The care she has taken of thee do thou in turn take of thy children."

up to the hilarity of a feast, when suddenly they were submerged in the waters of the Nile. On this intelligence the fury of their partisans broke out with such violence that Queen Nitocris could not withstand it. Her death became the signal for such sanguinary discords that, according to an ancient tradition, there were in Egypt seventy kings in seventy days.

FOUNDATION OF THEBES.—In the midst of the anarchy one of the princes who were contending for supremacy had founded Thebes, the capital of Upper Egypt, or Thèbaid. This city, owing to the victories of a king of the eleventh dynasty who extended his sway over all the country, soon became the capital of Egypt. Then began the erection of those famous structures which rendered Thebes one of the most beautiful cities in the world. Its hundred gates, sung by Homer, sufficiently attest its size and the number of its inhabitants. The poet asserts that from each of its gates could be sent forth two hundred chariots and ten thousand warriors. This is doubtless an exaggeration, but modern travellers certify that the magnificence of Thebes was commensurate with its extent. In the midst of its ruins, which cover a space of several leagues on both sides of the Nile, the spectator still beholds temples, palaces, and tombs, not less remarkable for the richness of their decorations than for their majestic proportions, and upon which are engraved the names of Egyptian kings and gods.

It is believed that the true God was first known at Thebes under the name of *Ammon*, or the "Invisible," who was adored as the "Lord of eternity," the "great God dwelling in truth"; but Thebes, "the holy city of Ammon," having adopted the worship of the stars and of animals, became the principal centre of idolatry in antiquity. As if to purify a country so long sullied by such an offence, God afterwards made it the cradle of the Christian religious life, in causing to flourish there the admirable virtues of St. Antony and other solitaries of the Thebaid.

GLORY OF THE MIDDLE EMPIRE UNDER THE TWELFTH DYNASTY; THE LABYRINTH.—Egypt, which already formed a single kingdom under the eleventh dynasty, recovered under the twelfth all the neighboring countries that she had lost during the civil wars. The princes of the twelfth dynasty also made new conquests in Ethiopia, while they became illustrious as the builders of those monuments which all agree in ranking among the masterpieces of Egyptian art. The most famous of all is the Labyrinth, in the ruins of which have recently been discovered the name and tomb of its founder, King Amenehme III.*

* The kings of the twelfth dynasty, who occupied the throne about two centuries, bore in turn the names of Amenehme and Osortasen. The most remarkable were Amenehme III., who founded the Laby-

It was not so much one single palace as a magnificent pile composed of twelve palaces, regularly disposed, which had communication with each other. Fifteen hundred rooms, interspersed with terraces, were ranged round twelve halls, and no outlet could be discovered by those who went to see them. There was the like number of buildings under ground. These subterranean structures were designed for the burying-place of the kings, and also, by a deplorable superstition, for keeping the sacred crocodiles, which the Egyptians, so wise in other respects, worshipped as gods.

INVASION OF THE HYKSOS.—Egypt, again rent by civil war and dismembered into several states, under the thirteenth dynasty suffered the invasion of the Hyksos, or shepherd-kings, from Syria and the neighboring states. "The breath of God's wrath," says the historian Manetho, "arises against us. Obscure men, appearing unawares from the side of the Orient, dared to invade our country, of which they made themselves masters without striking a blow. They subjugated the reigning princes, burnt cities, and overthrew temples and gods; they inflicted on the inhabitants every possible evil, slaughtering some, enslaving others with their wives and children."

rinth, which was completed or repaired in the seventh century B.C.; and Osortasen III., who conquered Nubia—*i.e.*, the northern part of Ethiopia, under which name the ancients also comprised Abyssinia and the neighboring countries as far as the equator.

———+———

The shepherd-kings remained masters of Egypt about three centuries. Establishing themselves in the lower valley of the Nile, they imposed tribute on the rest of the country. Their king resided sometimes at Memphis, and sometimes at Avaris (Pelūsiŭm), where he kept an army of 240,000 men. The last king of the Hyksos, named Apophis, raised Joseph to the dignity of prime minister, and settled the patriarch Jacob with all his family in the land of Gèssen.*

Sec. 2. NEW EMPIRE: *Conquests and Monuments of the Kings of the Eighteenth and Nineteenth Dynasties—Thoutmosis III. and Ramsēs II., or Sèsóstrīs.*

EXPULSION OF THE HYKSOS.—The kings of Thebes, compelled to pay tribute, had long failed in the attempt to recover their independence. Finally, about the year 1700 B. C., King Amosis succeeded in expelling the invaders, and hence was justly regarded as the head of the eighteenth dynasty and the founder of a new empire. At

---

* All recent discoveries agree with the Bible in maintaining that the last shepherd-kings had adopted the manners and language of Egypt. Thus, Joseph was sold to an officer named Putiphar—*i.e.*, "one who belongs to the sun"—and he received from the king the title of "foster-father of the world," or of the *country*, because the same Egyptian word (*to*) designated the world and Egypt, which was *the* country *par excellence*. As to the name Pharao, given by the Bible to the sovereign of Egypt, it properly signified *sun*, and by extension *king*, because the sovereign gloried in being the representative of the sun and in taking its name.

the head of an army of 480,000 men, after having driven the Hyksos as far as the environs of Avaris (Pelusium), Amosis took that place. The Hyksos, driven from Egypt, migrated, some to Arabia, others to Phœnicia, Syria, and Chanaan, afterwards called Palestine.

Amosis, desiring to prevent another invasion, pursued the vanquished to their own territory, and thus opened to his successors the way to Asia. King Thoutmosis I., master of Phœnicia and Chanaan, imposed tribute on Syria, and extended his conquests as far as Mesopotamia. This prince, who also subjugated Ethiopia, paved the way to the glorious reign of his second son, Thoutmosis III., the greatest of Egyptian conquerors.

ZENITH OF THE NEW EMPIRE UNDER THOUTMOSIS III.—Thoutmosis III., being still young when he ascended the throne, at first left the care of government to his eldest sister, Hatason. This princess evinced so much wisdom and firmness that during her life-time the tributary nations dared not raise the standard of revolt. After her death, however, the Syrians and Chanaanites threatened Egypt with a new invasion. Thoutmosis, marching to meet them, defeated them at Mageddo, in Palestine, compelled Syria to resume the yoke, and penetrated to the interior of Asia, where he imposed tribute on the kings of Ninive and Babylon. Even Armenia and all Arabia acknowledged the rule of the conqueror. At the same

time his vessels, manned by Phœnicians, subjugated the coasts of Asia Minor and Greece, the
isles of Cyprus and Crete, and facilitated the conquest of the African coast to Algeria. Egypt thus
became mistress of the then known world. Upon
one of the monuments erected at Thebes by King
Thoutmosis we read this eulogium, addressed to
him by the god Ammon: "I have rejoiced at beholding thy beauty, O my avenging son! I have
compelled the nations that I have humbled beneath thy hand to laud thy invincible majesty.
The East and the West lie at the foot of thy
throne. Thou hast been to the ends of the earth,
and all lands have heard thy shouts of victory."

AMENOPHIS III.; THE STATUE OF MEMNON.—
The vast empire of Thoutmosis III. lasted till his
third successor, Amenophis III., who is less celebrated for his military exploits than for the
number and magnificence of his monuments. At
Thebes is still seen his colossal statue, sixty feet in
height. It represents Pharao seated, his hands
extended on his knees, in an attitude of repose.
This statue sent forth at sunrise harmonious
sounds. The ancients, regarding this as a prodi-
gy, long asserted that it was the Ethiopian Memnon, one of the defenders of Troy, who every
morning thus saluted his mother, Aurora. But
the statue, being mutilated by an earthquake, and
afterwards repaired by the Emperor Septimius
Severus, became silent. It is now believed that

if the statue gave forth musical sounds, it was
owing to the sun's rays dilating the inner cham-
bers, which had been contracted by the coolness
of night.

RAMSÈS II., OR SESOSTRIS; HIS WARS AND
MONUMENTS.—The power of Egypt waned under
the successors of Amenophis III., but began to
revive under Ramses I., the head of the nineteenth dynasty.* Sethos I., son of Ramses,
pursued the policy of his father with such success that he regained all the conquests of Thoutmosis III. Hence this prince, as well for his
valor as for his love of art, merits to be ranked
among the most illustrious Pharaos. His glory,
however, was eclipsed by that which the Greeks
attribute to his son, Ramses II., so celebrated in
history as Sesostris.†

---

* The eighteenth dynasty, which had carried the power of Egypt
to its height, was extinguished, as so many others, amid the disasters
of civil war. Amenophis III. left several children, one of whom,
Amenophis IV., rendered himself odious by undertaking to reform the
ancient religion, and another, named Horus, had to struggle against
a great number of claimants. It is believed that at his death one
of these claimants became the head of the nineteenth dynasty,
under the name of Ramses, or "child of the son."

† The Greek historians Herodotus and Diodórus of Sicily, crediting
legendary accounts, have related that the father of Sesostris, design-
ing to fit his son to be a conqueror, caused him to be reared with all
the children that were born in Egypt on the same day as himself.
They were early inured to a hard and laborious life, to enable them
one day to sustain the fatigues of war. Scarcely had Sesostris
ascended the throne when he conceived the design of making the
conquest of the entire world, and to this end collected an army of
600,000 foot, 24,000 horse, and 27,000 armed war-chariots. According

—✠—

Sesostris, though long ranked as a great conqueror, undertook war only to preserve the conquests of his predecessors. He has left us a certain proof of this in the numerous inscriptions
in which his vanity parades in pompous terms
the minutest details of his military exploits.
After repressing a revolt of Ethiopia he waged a
long and desperate war against Syria and the
neighboring states, which had taken up arms at
the instigation of the Hetheans, the most warlike
of the Chanaanitish tribes. Victory remained
with Pharao, who was thus enabled to maintain
in Asia the Egyptian rule as he had received it
from his father, Sethos.

A better title to glory is the great number and
magnificence of the monuments that Sesostris
caused to be erected in the valley of the Nile,
from the city of Tanis to the extremity of Nubia.
In this respect he surpassed all the other Pharaos.
At Memphis and in Nubia are still to be seen
colossal statues, sixty-five feet in height, representing him seated on a throne. Thebes, however, was the city which Sesostris embellished
with the most remarkable structures. All
tourists who have visited the ruins agree in say-

to the same historians, he subjugated Ethiopia, Arabia, and other
countries which had already been conquered by his predecessors.
Besides, he traversed as conqueror Persia, India, Colchis, Scythia to
the Tanais, Asia Minor, and Thrace—a country which none of the
Pharaos ever penetrated, for it is certain that the most warlike did
not go beyond the Tigris and Armenia.

ing that they present a most wonderful spectacle.*

GOVERNMENT OF SESOSTRIS.—Sesostris, were we to credit the Greeks, joined to the glory of a conqueror that of a wise legislator, securing by equitable measures the happiness and prosperity of Egypt. But the best laws of Egypt existed before his accession, and he applied himself less to enforce them than to gratify his vanity. He . imposed the most tyrannical labors on the people. Not content with employing on his structures all the prisoners of war, he tore from their homes many families of the tributary provinces, and sent troops to hunt negroes in the south of Ethiopia. It is at present a received opinion that Sesostris is that Pharao of the Bible who condemned the

* The principal monuments of Thebes are those of Karnak and Luxor, upon the right bank of the Nile; those of Rameseum, of Gournah, and of Medinet-Abou, on the left bank. Among the monuments of Karnak, in the erection of which all the kings of the eighteenth dynasty engaged, is a vast hall (attributed to Sethos I.), 319 feet long, 150 wide, and adorned with 130 columns, each 70 feet high. Sesostris finished the structures of Karnak; enlarged those of Luxor, began by Amenophis III.; built the Rameseum (so called from his name, Ramses); erected a palace at Medinet-Abou, and embellished Gournah, the principal necropolis of Thebes. Before the temple of Luxor he caused to be erected, according to the custom, two obelisks, one of which has been transported to the Place de la Concorde, at Paris. This obelisk, hewn from a single piece of red granite, is seventy-two feet high. Its four sides are covered with sixteen hundred hieroglyphic characters. On the western side is seen Sesostris, offering wine to the god Ammon. Pharao there bears his surname of *Meriamoun*, or "beloved of Ammon," and he is proclaimed "the chosen son of the king of the gods, who from the height of his throne rules the whole world."

Hebrews to the most painful labors, and who ordained the death of their new-born babes. It is at least known that the Egyptians were reduced to a very wretched condition. The chief librarian of Sesostris, in a letter to his friend Pentaour, thus depicts it : "Before the husbandman has reaped, insects destroy a part of his harvest. If he neglects to take in what he has reaped, robbers seize it from him in the fields. The tax-gatherer appears in a district, bringing with him minions armed with rods, and negroes with palm branches, saying, 'Give us your wheat,' and there is no means of eluding their exactions. Finally, the wretched victim is seized, bound, and sent to labor at the canals."

MISERABLE END OF THE NINETEENTH DYNASTY.—Sesostris at his death, after a reign of sixty-five years, left Egypt exhausted by his tyranny, and overrun by barbarians whom he had not been able to repulse. The Italians and Greeks, having made themselves masters of Libya, invaded Lower Egypt. Their audacity augmenting with their success, they ascended the Nile, ravaging both shores of the river. Their approach put to flight the son and successor of Sesostris, called Merenphtah—i.e., "beloved of Phtah," the god of Memphis. An Egyptian general, braver and more skilful than Pharao, vanquished the barbarians and delivered Egypt.

—✦—

But a more terrible war soon broke out. Merenphtah had the imprudence to collect at Pelusium "all the lepers and the impure" of his kingdom. These wretched creatures, to the number of 80,000, took up arms and were reinforced by 200,000 foreigners from Asia. For thirteen years their implacable hatred caused Egypt to suffer all manner of calamities, during which Merenphtah disappeared. His son, a fugitive in Ethiopia, took the name of Sethos II., and reclaimed his paternal inheritance; but he had to struggle with competitors, and the nineteenth dynasty terminated miserably. It seems to have suffered the just retribution of its cruelty for being the first and most notorious persecutor of the people of God.*

Sec. 3. DECLINE OF THE NEW EMPIRE:
Ethiopian Kings (725–665 B.C.) *and Saïte Kings* (665–525 B.C.) *; Conquest of Egypt by Cambyses* (525 B.C.) *; Institutions and Manners of the Egyptians.*

ANARCHY: THE HIGH-PRIEST OF AMMON AND

---

* Most critics at present agree that Merenphtah, son of Sesostris, is the Pharao of the Bible who, by his obduracy, caused the ten plagues of Egypt, and who finally permitted Moses to lead the Hebrews out of his kingdom. Some critics place the exodus under the father of Sesostris; others under Horus, the last son of Amenophis III. None of these conjectures has as yet been verified. Notwithstanding the clear and precise account of the Bible, its coincidence with the history of Egypt has not yet been settled. This is due to the vanity of the Pharaos, which never suffered them to place on their monuments any testimony of their errors or reverses.

—+—

THE KINGS OF LOWER EGYPT.—About the close
of the twentieth dynasty the valor of Ramses III.
shed new lustre over the empire of the Pharaos.
His victories over the Libyan and Syrian nations
enabled him to bequeath to his successors all the
ancient conquests of Egypt; but they, inheriting
none of his talents, allowed the high-priest of
Ammon to usurp little by little the civil and military power.   About the year 1150 B.C. this ambitious priest consummated his usurpation, as did
the mayors of the palace in France, by assuming
the title of king.   But he was obliged to combat
a rival dynasty established at Tanis, in Lower
Egypt.   To securely establish himself in power,
the high-priest sought the alliance of the Assyrian
kings, and renounced the right of sovereignty
that Egypt during five centuries had exercised in
Asia, even beyond the Euphrates.

Egypt being thus weakened and divided, King
David was enabled, with little difficulty, to en-
large his kingdom at the expense of the neighboring smaller states.   His son Solomon was so
powerful that Pharao considered himself honored
in having him for a son-in-law.   But the schism
of the ten tribes divided Israel into two kingdoms,
whilst the Pharaos of Lower Egypt compelled the
descendants of the high-priest to flee into Ethiopia.   Acting at the instigation of Jeroboam,
Sesac, master of all Egypt, invaded the kingdom
of Juda (971)   A prophet announced that he

EGYPT. 29

was but the instrument of divine vengeance. Entering Jerusalem, he pillaged the palace of Roboam and seized the treasures of the Temple. We still see among the monuments of Karnak a bas-relief representing this first triumph of the Egyptians over the people of God.

THE ETHIOPIAN KINGS AND THE ASSYRIAN INVASION (725–665).—The descendants of the high-priest, having taken refuge in Ethiopia, established there an independent kingdom. One of them, named Zara, placing himself at the head of an immense army, invaded both Egypt and the kingdom of Juda. God told the holy king Asa that he would be victorious, and the Ethiopians were vanquished. Egypt, too, would have recovered her independence had she not been divided into many hostile states. Favored by this anarchy, the Ethiopian king, Sabacon, descended the valley of the Nile and subdued nearly the whole country. Then the Jews, menaced by the Assyrian armies, sought the alliance of Egypt, regardless of the prophet Isaias : "Woe to them that go down to Egypt for help . . . and have not trusted in the Holy One of Israel. The princes of Tanis are confounded, the princes of Memphis have wandered away. I will deliver Egypt into the hands of cruel masters, and a strong king shall rule over them." And the prophet, walking barefoot with his garments disordered, cried out : "So shall the king of the

Assyrians lead away the prisoners cf Egypt and the captivity of Ethiopia."

The prophecy was literally fulfilled. The new Egyptian allies neither prevented the ruin of the kingdom of Israel nor hindered the march of Sennacherib. Egypt, likewise invaded, remained exposed to the attacks of the Assyrians, who covered with blood and ruin the banks of the Nile.

THE TWELVE KINGS (665–650).—After a long period of anarchy twelve of the principal Egyptian chiefs agreed to reign together, with the title of kings (665). Their union lasted fifteen years, and it is believed that, to testify this to posterity, they built, at their common expense, the famous Labyrinth of Memphis. But, according to Herodotus, an oracle had declared that he who would offer his libations iu a brazen vase should eventually become master of Egypt. One day, as they were offering sacrifice together, there happening to be but eleven golden cups, one of them, Psammeticus, used as a cup his helmet, which was of brass. The others, remembering the oracle and fearing its fulfilment, deposed their colleague, who fled to the marshes at the mouth of the Nile.

THE SAÏTE KINGS; PSAMMETICUS (650–616).— According to Herodotus, Psammeticus learned that an oracle had decreed that men of brass would come from the sea to avenge him. Some time after he saw Greek pirates disembark, clad in brazen armor. Having gained them over to his cause, he dethroned the eleven other kings, his persecutors, and drove the Ethiopians from the Thebaid. Being thus master of Egypt, and wishing to render his dynasty illustrious, he called it Saïs, because his father had reigned in that city of the Delta. The new Pharao, after having refused to acknowledge the supremacy of Assyria, still aspired to re-establish in Asia the ancient power of Egypt. As he relied on the courage of the Greeks for that enterprise, he attracted a great number to his kingdom, favoring them, even to the detriment of his native warriors, two hundred thousand of whom emigrated to Ethiopia. Psammeticus felt that this loss would be fatal to his power. Having besieged Azoth, a city of the Philistines, he took it after twenty-eight years. This is the longest siege known in antiquity.

NECHAO (616–600).—Nechao, adopting the policy of his father, placed himself at the head of a powerful army, resolved to carry the war to the Euphrates. Already master of the country of the Philistines, he endeavored to pass the frontiers of the kingdom of Juda. King Josias, viewing this with suspicion, wished to prevent his passage. Rejecting the protestations of friendship made by Pharao, he gave battle at Mageddo, in the plain of Esdrelon. Josias was defeated and

killed (610). The conqueror took Jerusalem and
imposed tribute on Juda. After subduing Syria
Pharao advanced to the Euphrates, where he met
the great Nabuchodonosor. Defeated at Circesium, Nechao lost in one day all his conquests
(604).

Nechao was not more prosperous in his design
of increasing Egyptian commerce. He attempted
to reopen the canal which his father, Sesostris,
had caused to be dug between the Nile and
the Red Sea. This enterprise cost the lives of
120,000 workmen, and the king, warned by an
oracle that he was laboring for the barbarians,
desisted from the attempt. It was at his instigation that the Phœnician mariners made the
tour of Africa and returned to Egypt through
the strait of Hercules. But this voyage, which
lasted three years, led to no important result.

PSAMMIS (600–594) AND APRIES (594–569);
USURPATION OF AMASIS (569–526).—Psammis,
after an unfruitful expedition into Ethiopia, left
the crown to his son Apries, called Ophra in the
Bible, because of his Egyptian name, which sig-
nifies "the son enlarges his heart." This ambitious prince, having seized the city of Sidon, was
so filled with pride that he dared defy Heaven to
shake his throne. As he wished to avenge the
defeat of his grandfather at Circesium, he offered
the Jews his protection against Nabuchodonosor.
Sedecias, last king of Juda, imprudently accepted

the offer, despite the terrible menace of Jeremias and Ezechiel. These two prophets, in the name of God, forbade the king to rely upon Egypt, equally criminal and weak, likening her to a frail reed, which, breaking under the hand, wounds instead of sustaining. In fact, the Pharao Ophra, after a vain show, fled before the Babylonians, who spent all their fury on King Sedecias and the city of Jerusalem (587).

Jeremias, to prove his divine mission, had predicted the tragic end of Pharao · "Thus saith the Lord: Behold I will deliver Pharao Ophra, King of Egypt, into the hand of his enemies and into the hand of them that seek his life." Pharao, hearing of the revolt of his troops in Libya, charged an officer named Amasis to bring them back to their duty. But Amasis, being proclaimed king by the rebels, marched against his master, made him prisoner, and delivered him into the hands of the furious populace, who strangled him.

The new Pharao was of low birth. Wishing to conciliate the esteem and respect of the Egyptians, he pandered to their superstitious practices. He had a golden vessel in which he washed his feet before going to the table; melting it down, he had it cast into a statue. The people hastened in crowds to adore the new statue, when the king informed them of the vile uses to which this statue, now the object of their religious veneration, had been put. The application of his words was easy and had the desired effect; the people thenceforward paid the king all the respect due to his majesty. The usurper by wise measures assured the prosperity of Egypt. It contained during his reign, says Herodotus, twenty thousand flourishing cities. Amasis also imposed tribute on the Isle of Cyprus. But in favoring the Greeks he displeased the Egyptians, and, by making an alliance with the enemies of Cyrus, he provoked a formidable war, which burst forth during the reign of his son Psammenitus.

PSAMMENITUS (526–525); CONQUEST OF EGYPT BY CAMBYSES (525).—Cambyses, son of Cyrus, advanced upon Egypt under the pretext that alliances had been formed against the Persians, but in reality because he coveted the riches of that country. His army traversed without difficulty the desert, where the Arabs were employed in carrying to him vast supplies of water. Arriving at the frontiers of Egypt, he found the troops of Psammenitus ranged under the walls of Pelusium, ready to give battle. To hasten the capture of the place the Persian king made use of a singular stratagem. He placed in the van of his army a great number of cats, dogs, and other animals held as sacred by the Egyptians. The soldiers of Psammenitus dared not fling a dart that way for fear of hitting some of these animals. The Egyptians were utterly routed; the king fled to Memphis, but was pursued, made prisoner, and shortly after put to death. Such was the unhappy end of the most ancient and flourishing empire of the world.

RELIGION of the Egyptians; *The Bull Apis; the Mummies and the Judgment of the Dead; King and Government; Priests, Warriors, and People; Laws; Sciences and Arts; Hieroglyphic Writing.*

RELIGION.—The Egyptians, enlightened by primitive revelation, acknowledged the true God, whom they declared one, all-powerful, eternal, maker of heaven and earth, and who, self-existing, remains invisible in his essence. But his power and other attributes were little by little confounded with the creatures which are but their manifestations, and hence resulted the grossest idolatry. The sun, the most glorious symbol of the goodness of God, was adored, under various appellations, as the Supreme Being, which gave life to all other beings, and more especially to certain animals useful or common in Egypt. Thus, the Egyptians ranked among their gods the ox, cow, sheep, cat, ape, hawk, crocodile, hippopotamus, ibis, and a number of other animals, which had each their sanctuary, their priest, and their burial-places. "If you enter a temple," says St. Clement of Alexandria, "a priest advances with a grave aspect singing a sacred hymn. He raises the veil a little, in order that you may see the god. What do you see? A cat, a crocodile, a serpent, or some other dangerous animal. Behold the god of the Egyptians! It is but a wild beast wallowing on a carpet of purple."

THE BULL APIS.—Of all these deities the bull Apis was the most famous. Magnificent temples were erected to him; extraordinary honors were paid him. The Egyptians did not, however, permit him to live too long; for if he attained his twenty-fifth year, they drowned him in the waters of the Nile. At his death Egypt went into general mourning. After the last honors had been paid to the deceased god the next care was to find him a successor, which was known by certain marks. As soon as one was found he was conducted to Memphis amidst general rejoicings. It is probable that the golden calf set up by the Israelites was an imitation of the god Apis, as well as those afterwards set up by Jeroboam, King of Israel, at the extremities of his kingdom, for this prince had resided a considerable time in Egypt. It was perhaps to show what man is when abandoned to himself that God permitted a nation where human wisdom was carried to the highest degree among the ancients thus blindly to abandon itself to the most gross and ridiculous superstitions. *

* The Serapeum of Memphis was discovered in 1854 to have been

THE MUMMIES AND THE JUDGMENT OF THE DEAD.—The Egyptians believed in the immortality of the soul, and consequently in the rewards and punishments of a future life. This belief appears to have changed into that of metempsychosis—that is, the transmigration of the soul from one body into that of another after death; but they retained the custom of giving that care to the body which they deemed necessary for its happiness in the future life. When the relations had mourned the deceased, they gave the body over to the embalmers. This process, always performed with rare skilfulness, occupied about seventy days. The body having been thoroughly saturated with various liquids and aromatics, was washed, swathed in linen fillets, and placed in a sycamore chest. In this condition they have been preserved for thousands of years, and have received the name of mummies. (Egypt has a dry and nitrous soil, well adapted for the preservation of the dead. Some grains of wheat found near a mummy, where they had lain for more than three thousand years, were carried to Europe and sown. They germinated, and produced the ancient wheat of Egypt.) Everything having been prepared for

the burial-place of the bulls Apis. One of these animals, which died in the reign of Ramses II., or Sesostris, was honored with this inscription : "Here lies Osiris-Apis, who resides in Paradise; the great god, the eternal lord, the master for ever."

the funeral obsequies, the relations fixed the day, following the ancient custom of convening judges, accusers, and the friends of the deceased. "Each one must pass the lake of the province where he died." The judges, numbering more than forty, sat in a semicircle on the shore of the lake. There, in the presence of the dead, the public accuser was heard. If it was proved that the deceased had led a bad life, his memory was condemned and he was deprived of burial. If the accusation was unjust, he who made it was condemned to pay a heavy fine. If the deceased was convicted of no crime, he was honorably interred, and all the people with loud acclamations besought the gods to admit him as a partaker with them of their everlasting felicity.

The relations placed the body in the family vault, sometimes upright against the wall, but oftener in an ornamented niche.* As to the soul of the deceased, it was supposed to make a long and perilous voyage, at the end of which it was to undergo many trials and have all its actions weighed in the balance of justice.

THE KING AND HIS GOVERNMENT.—Egypt was governed by a king who prided himself on being the son of the sun, and his image among

* "The Egyptians," says Diodorus of Sicily, " called their houses inns, as man abode therein but for a short time ; but their tombs were called mansions, for the body remained there during a succession of ages. They therefore built magnificent sepulchres, and adorned their houses but little."

the living. His subjects adored and respected
him as a god. Despite the prestige of an authority without limit, he was nevertheless subjected to the religious laws of his country, which
regulated his conduct even to the minutest particular. At his death the crown passed, by law
of primogeniture, first to his sons, then to his
daughters, and, if he had no.direct descendants,
to his brothers and sisters. His court was composed of numerous functionaries, for his own service and that of the government. To render the
administration easier, Egypt was divided into for-
ty-four districts. Each district had its governor, who was aided by subaltern officers. All the
land of each district was recorded in a register
and divided into three categories, according to
the nature of its products; the canals furnished
fish, the plains cereals, and the marshes cattle.
All imposts were paid in kind, since the use of
money was unknown in Egypt. Commerce was
carried on by exchange, or by ingots whose value
was reckoned by their weight.

THE PRIESTS, THE WARRIORS, AND THE PEO-
PLE.—There were in Egypt two privileged
classes, the one of priests and the other of warriors, each possessing a third of the soil. The
first, which was always held in great esteem, was
sufficiently powerful to overthrow the twentieth
dynasty. The second lost all its influence when
two hundred thousand warriors retired to Etho-

——+——

pia rather than fight in the service of Psammeticus. The people formed the third class in the
state. They consisted principally of agriculturists and shepherds, because those two avocations
were regarded as the most useful to man, since
they furnish him with the fruits of the earth and
the animals that it nourishes ; but these agriculturists were but tillers, since all the land belonged either to the king or to the two privileged
classes, and the permanent shepherds alone were
esteemed by the Egyptians, who detested the
nomadic habits of the neighboring tribes. They
had besides a great number of artisans, who
worked the metals, made glass, porcelain, and
all kinds of stuffs. The Egyptians wore linen
garments bordered with fringe, and over this a
large mantle of white wool. Their constitution
was robust, which they attributed to their so-
briety. "They made their bread," says an historian, "with spelt, or bearded wheat; they
drank beer and fed on birds and fish, except
those that were considered sacred ; they ate them
roasted or boiled, or merely dipped into brine
and dried in the sun. It was one of their
maxims that in our repasts are found the sources
of all maladies."

EGYPTIAN LAWS.—"Egypt," says Bossuet,
"was the source of all good government. God
designed that Moses should be skilled in all the
wisdom of the Egyptians." That wisdom con-

sisted principally in conforming their laws and customs to the principles of natural equity, which so excited the admiration of strangers that Pythagoras, Lycurgus, Solon, Plato, and all the greatest philosophers and legislators of antiquity came to study in her school.

"Perjury," says Diodorus of Sicily, "was punished with death, because it combines the two greatest crimes, one against the gods and the other against man. The author of a false accusation, if unmasked, was subjected to a heavy penalty. Every Egyptian was obliged to render to the magistrate a written account of his means of subsistence; if his declaration was false, or if he gained his livelihood by unlawful means, he was condemned to death. An Egyptian could borrow only by giving as a pledge the mummy of his father. If he failed to pay the debt, he was deprived of the right of sepulture."

These laws with a host of others formed the basis of religion, society, family, and property. To insure their execution upright judges were chosen from sacerdotal families. The president of the tribunal wore on his neck a chain of gold, to which was suspended an image of Truth. All the affairs of justice were transacted in writing, never orally, lest the powers of eloquence by exciting the passions might cause partiality among the judges.

SCIENCE AND ARTS.—The Egyptians success-

—✛—

fully cultivated geometry, which was indispensable for surveying lands, for cutting stone, and for the construction of monuments. Their knowledge of astronomy is shown by their discovering the solar year to be of 365 days, and also by their determining with precision the four cardinal points. But we learn with surprise that their machinery was confined to the lever, the inclined plane, and, above all, the human arm, to transport the most enormous masses. One hundred and twenty thousand men were necessary to erect one of the obelisks of Thebes.

Recent discoveries prove that the Egyptians, even under the first dynasties, painted and carved with as much delicacy as naturalness. The distinctive character of their art, however, consisted in the gigantic and majestic proportions of their statues and their monuments. It is said with reason that because religion inspired them to honor their gods, their kings, and their dead, their works have a superhuman grandeur and seem made for eternity. We have already mentioned the palaces, the temples, and the most remarkable tombs. It remains to speak of a kind of statue very common in Egypt—*i.e.*, the sphinx, which consists of a human head placed on the body of a lion couchant with outstretched paws. We have here an emblem of divinity and royalty. The most colossal sphinx is found near the large pyramids, and dates from the reign of Chephrem, its head alone being twenty-six feet from the chin to the crown.

HIEROGLYPHIC WRITING.—All the monuments of Egypt bear written inscriptions which are called hieroglyphs, or sacred characters, for they were long thought to be mysterious signs known only to the Egyptian priests. The ancients did not transmit to us the key to their writings, and it was not till 1822 that it was found, thanks to the acuteness of a learned Frenchman, J. F. Champollion. We now know that these hieroglyphs were familiar to most Egyptians, and that they could decipher them by means of a very complicated alphabet. Besides the signs which represent letters or syllables, a great number represent either the objects themselves—as a circle or a crescent for the sun and moon—or the idea that the objects form in the mind; thus, a lion for courage, a sparrow-hawk for speed. So, also, the Egyptians represented a son by a goose, the idea of justice by a feather of an ostrich; because they thought the first of these birds a model of filial piety, and the feathers of the latter are exactly equal.

The Egyptians had also a cursive writing, called hieratic, which was an abbreviation of the hieroglyphic. This they wrote on the inner bark of the plant called papyrus; hence the name paper.

There have been discovered in our times many

very ancient books written on papyrus, and though, perhaps, they do not suffice to enable us to appreciate those libraries styled the " Treasury of the remedies of the soul," they yet furnish us with a new proof that the Egyptians preceded all other people in the culture of letters and the arts.

REVIEW QUESTIONS.

What is said of the ancient history of Egypt ? Name the periods into which it is divided. By whom was Egypt peopled ? What of Menes ? Describe the inundation of the Nile. The pyramids, why were they erected ? Describe Lake Mœris. What of Queen Nitocris? By whom was Thebes founded ? Describe it. Of what the Thebaid the cradle ? Describe the Labyrinth. What were kept in it ? Who were the Hyksos ? How long did they remain ? What of the last king ? When and by whom were they expelled ? What of Thoutmosis III. ? Describe the statue of Memnon. Who was Sesostris ? What of his wars ? His monuments ? His government ? How did the nineteenth dynasty end ? What of Ramses III. ? King David ? Solomon ? By whom was Juda invaded ? What of the prophet Isaias ? When did the twelve kings reign ? What of Psammeticus ? Of Nechao ? Of Psammis ? Of Amasis ? What did Jeremias predict ? Describe the conquest of Egypt by Cambyses. What of the superstitions of the Egyptians ? What says St. Clement of Alexandria ? What of Apis ? What are mummies ? Describe the judgment of the dead. How was Egypt governed ? Into how many classes were the people divided ? Describe each. What does Bossuet say of the laws of Egypt ? How was perjury regarded ? What knowledge did the Egyptians have of the arts and sciences ? What was the sphinx ? How many modes of writing did the Egyptians use ? Describe the hieroglyphic. The hieratic. In what did the Egyptians precede all other people ?

CHAPTER II.

ASSYRIA AND BABYLON.

THE history of Assyria and Babylon comprises two periods: the first from the foundation of Babylon and Ninive to the ruin of Ninive and the second Assyrian Empire (625 B.C.); the second from the Babylonian or Chaldean Empire to the taking of Babylon by Cyrus (625–538 B.C.)

Sec. 1. **BABYLON AND NINIVE**: *First Assyrian Empire* (1314–789 B.C.); *Salmanasar IV.* (905–871 B.C.); *Second Assyrian Empire* (744–625 B.C.); *Sennacherib* (704–681 B.C.)

BABYLON AND NINIVE.—After the dispersion of mankind Nimrod, grandson of Cham, laid the foundations of Babylon, at the foot of the Tower of Babel. Scripture informs us that he was a "mighty hunter." After destroying many wild beasts, he declared war against man, and was the first who aspired to the title of conqueror. His power appears to have been equalled by that of Assur, son of Sem, who built on the left bank of the Tigris' the famous Ninive, the rival of Babylon, and for a long time her ruler.

These two cities were at first the capitals of two small, independent kingdoms. We learn from the Bible that their empire did not extend

over the other important cities situated near the
Euphrates, among which was (Ur of Chaldea,
where Abram was born.) It is, therefore, believed that the country was divided into several
states, sometimes at war, sometimes leagued
against one another. (This explains how Abram,
with his three hundred and eighteen servants,
could disperse the army of the four kings who had
made his nephew prisoner.) And it is certain that
the Chaldeans, masters of Babylon, soon after
extended their sway over Ninive and other cities
washed by the Tigris and Euphrates. Inscriptions have been discovered attesting the power of
the Chaldean monarchs. (Their empire lasted
till the seventeenth century B.C., when the
Pharaos, advancing to the Euphrates, reduced
the kings of Babylon and Ninive to mere vassals
of Egypt.)

FOUNDATION OF THE FIRST ASSYRIAN EMPIRE
(1314); TIGLATH-PILESER I. (ABOUT 1100).—As
the suzerainty of Egypt became purely nominal
under the successors of Sesostris, the kings of
Ninive profited by this to extend by degrees their
conquests towards the Euphrates. One of them,
named (Tiglath-samdan,) occupied Babylon and
founded the first Assyrian or Ninivite Empire
(1314).* This prince, according to the custom

---

* According to Ctesias, a Greek historian of the fourth century,
Ninus, second founder of Ninive, had conquered Babylon and all the
cities lying between the Mediterranean and the Indus. It was in

in Asia, left the crown to the kings of Babylon, on condition that they would pay tribute. They made many attempts to recover their independence, and these revolts always ended in bloody wars. The Assyrian monarchs, from the first victorious, at length became invincible, and the Pharaos, releasing them from vassalage, esteemed themselves fortunate in obtaining their alliance and support.

(Tiglath-pileser was the first who aspired to the conquest of Western Asia.) After conquering the countries bordering upon the Caspian and Euxine Seas, he crossed the Euphrates, seized Circesium, and defeated the Hethians, who had long been the implacable enemies of Egypt. It was then easy to penetrate into Phœnicia, where he wished to embark on the Mediterranean, which had never before been done by any of his predecessors. The monarch glorified himself in an inscription as having "slain with his own hand a dolphin," and with having received shortly after, from the king of Egypt, "as an extra-

---

Bactriana that he espoused Semiramis, because of her courage. Semiramis, after the death of Ninus, enlarged Babylon, marched triumphantly through Media, Persia, and Western Asia ; she also conquered Egypt and Ethiopia, but, after an unfortunate expedition into India, she abdicated the throne in favor of her son Ninyas, having reigned forty-two years. This narrative of Ctesias is not accepted by critics, and is refuted by other historians and by the recently-discovered monuments. There is no other historical Semiramis than the wife of Belochus III., about the year 800.

ordinary present, a crocodile from his river and whales from the great sea."

The Jews were not disturbed by the great conqueror who had defeated the neighboring nations. It was at this period that God destined David to found a great kingdom in Western Asia. He therefore ordained that Tiglath-pileser, after having completed his plan, should be recalled to the Euphrates by a fresh revolt of Babylon, which caused him great embarrassment and resulted in the loss of all his conquests.

ZENITH OF THE FIRST ASSYRIAN EMPIRE; SARDANAPALUS III. (930–905) AND SALMANASAR IV. (905–870).—The Assyrian Empire, weakened for a century and a half, recovered its power only to become the instrument of divine justice against the idolatrous kingdoms of Juda and Israel. ("Assyria," said the Lord, "is the rod of my anger, and I will revenge myself by its hands.") (Sardanapalus III. began this work of vengeance by recovering all the conquests of Tiglath-pileser. He added to them Media, and went in person to impose tribute on the Phœnician cities. Everywhere he left in his passage traces of his cruelty. He caused his prisoners to be flayed alive, destroyed cities, and placed over them this inscription: "I smile over ruins, I joy in glutting my fury." His statue, which has been transported to London, represents him standing, holding in one hand a scythe, in the other a club, and

—✠—

bearing written on his breast the following pompous eulogy: " Sardanapalus, great king, powerful king, king of the legions, king of Assyria. He possessed the land from the river Tigris to Libanus; he subjected to his sway the great seas and all the countries from the rising to the setting of the sun."

His son, Salmanasar IV., inherited his power and employed it against the kings of Israel. In the narrative of his first campaign in Syria he himself mentions among the vanquished the impious Achab. Some years later, King Jehu having imprudently implored his aid, Salmanasar compelled him to pay tribute. On an obelisk recently discovered the Assyrian king enumerates all the precious articles he received in gold and silver, and the king of Israel is represented prostrate, with his face to the earth, before him, in the posture of a vassal. Salmanasar has left us the recital of his thirty-one campaigns, which rendered him master of a great part of Asia. His empire extended from Persia to the Euxine Sea, from Oxus to the country of the Philistines. This powerful monarch, surprised by a revolt of his younger son, died during the siege of his capital. His inheritance passed first to his elder son, then to his grandson, Belochus III., less celebrated for his military exploits than for the genius of his wife, Semiramis. This princess, according to the testimony of Herodotus, embellished Babylon and raised the famous dikes which preserved the lower plains of Mesopotamia from the inundation of the waters of the Euphrates. Her glory was such that on the Assyrian monuments we find the name of no other queen save the wife of Belochus.)

SARDANAPALUS V. ; FALL OF THE FIRST ASSYRIAN EMPIRE (789).—The Assyrian Empire, composed of turbulent subjects, could exist only by force of arms. In place of a warlike chieftain, the Assyrians found but an indolent and voluptuous master in Sardanapalus. It is related that this monarch spent his life among the women of his household, whose dress and occupations he assumed, even plying the spindle and distaff. (Arbaces, governor of the Medes, having one day observed the king engaged in some menial occupation, conceived the design of exciting his troops to revolt.) Phul, prince of Babylon, and many other chiefs, seconded him with all their forces. The rebels, defeated in three encounters, lost courage, but Phul reassured them by promising that if they would wait five days they should receive reinforcements. Aid arrived and secured them the victory. (Sardanapalus, shut up in Ninive, thought he had naught to fear inside its walls, for he deemed them strong enough to defy all the missiles of the besiegers.) (An oracle had declared that the city would be impregnable till the river became its enemy. The siege lasted two years, when, after prolonged rains, the waters of the Tigris inundated a great part of the city and overthrew the wall to the extent of a league.) (Then the king, persuaded that the prophecy was accomplished, erected in his palace a vast funeral pile, on which himself, his wives, and his treasures were consumed. The besiegers, after pillaging Ninive, consigned everything to fire and sword.*

SECOND ASSYRIAN EMPIRE; TIGLATH-PILE-SER II. (744–727).—Phul, surnamed *Belesis*, or "The Terrible," reduced Assyria to a dependency of Babylon. To obtain his alliance, the cruel Manahem, King of Israel, agreed to pay him a tribute of one thousand talents. The Assyrians, at the close of a long revolt, recovered their independence. Tiglath-pileser II., father of Sardanapalus V., founded the second Assyrian or Ninivite Empire (744). Several prosperous campaigns made him master of nearly all the inheritance of his ancestors. The impious Achaz, King of Juda, called him to his aid against the kings of Israel and Damascus. Tiglath-pileser, in return for his protection, obliged Achaz to

---

* Some maintain that the following was the epitaph of Sardanapa-lus, composed by himself :

"I have done nothing but eat, drink, and amuse myself.
   All else I counted as naught "

—an epitaph more worthy, they say, of a beast than of a man. But the best authorities assure us that the Greeks have confounded Sardanapalus V. with another king of the same name, and the siege of 789 with that of 625 which was followed by the destruction of Ninive

acknowledge himself his vassal, and to give over to him all the treasures of the Temple of Jerusalem. Then were accomplished the prophecies of Isaias and Amos: the kingdom of Damascus, called also Syria, was destroyed, the half of the kingdom of Israel was occupied by the conqueror, and the other half condemned to pay an onerous tribute. It is thought that Tiglath-pileser gave the first example of the barbarous policy—adopted by his successors—of transporting the entire conquered nation to the interior of his empire and replacing them by his own subjects. This was the beginning of the captivity of the ten tribes (721).

SALMANASAR VI. (727–722) AND SARGON (721–704); TAKING OF SAMARIA (718).—The prophet Isaias, scandalized at the crimes and idolatry of the Israelites, foretold to them: "The Lord shall bring upon thee, and upon thy people, and upon the house of thy father, days that have not come since the time of the separation of Ephraim from Juda with the king of the Assyrians. And it shall come to pass in that day, that the Lord shall hiss for the fly, that is in the uttermost part of the rivers of Egypt, and for the bee that is in the land of Assyria." Notwithstanding these terrible threats, Osee, King of Israel, made an alliance with the king of Egypt and refused to pay tribute to the Assyrians. Salmanasar besieged Samaria, but died before it was taken, when Sargon (mentioned in Isaias), the general of his troops, usurped the crown, took Samaria, and sent the ten tribes captive to Assyria. Tobias, one of the exiles, gained the good-will of the king and used his influence to better the lot of his brethren. A large number of strangers, transported from the shores of the Tigris to the environs of Samaria, mingling pagan rites with the law of Moses, formed a new people, known by the name of Samaritans.

Sargon defeated the king of Egypt at Raphia, in Palestine, but failed to capture Tyre, which he was not able to blockade by sea. His rule, however, extended from the Mediterranean shore to the isle of Cyprus. A great victory over the Chaldeans opened to him the gates of Babylon (709), when he retaliated the evils inflicted upon Ninive twenty years before. In short, after subjugating all the countries of Asia from Cilicia to the frontiers of India, this invincible conqueror, who boasted of having forced three hundred and fifty kings to adore his god Bel, fell by the poniard of an assassin.

SENNACHERIB (704–681) AND EZECHIAS.— Sennacherib undertook to treat the kingdom of Juda as his father had treated that of Israel. The holy King Ezechias at first hoped to resist him with the aid of the Egyptians and Philistines ; but Sennacherib, having crushed his allies, invaded and devastated Juda. "As to Ezechias," he himself says in an inscription, "I will shut him up in Jerusalem, the city of his greatness, as a bird in a cage. I will invest and blockade all the forts around the city. Then the fear of my majesty shall terrify Ezechias, King of Juda." The holy king consented to pay a considerable tribute in gold and silver; but this, instead of appeasing his ferocious enemy, made him still more intractable. It was then that God visibly took up his defence, charging the prophet Isaias to announce to him his speedy deliverance and the terrible chastisement of Sennacherib: ("When thou wast mad against me, thy pride came up to my ears: therefore I will put a ring in thy nose, and a bit between thy lips, and I will turn thee back by the way by which thou camest.") The following night the exterminating angel, passing through the Assyrian camp, slew 180,000 men. Sennacherib was obliged to fly, and to return, covered with shame, before those nations which had shortly before beheld him so haughty and menacing. The vengeance of Heaven pursued this impious prince even to Ninive, where he was slain in a temple of his idols by two of his sons, who, after that horrible parricide, took refuge in Armenia.

ASSAR-HADDON (681–667) AND SARDANAPALUS VI. (667–647).—Assar-Haddon, the fourth son of Sennacherib, profited by the crime of his brothers to seize the crown. After taking Sidon and ravaging all Phœnicia, he invaded the kingdom of Juda. King Manasses, by his idolatry and cruelty, had drawn upon himself and his people the anger of God. (Made prisoner in Jerusalem, he was carried captive to Babylon, where he passed many years in the depths of a dungeon.) Assar-Haddon restored him to liberty only on condition that he should pay tribute. This indefatigable conqueror, having subjugated all of Arabia, spread like a torrent over Egypt, which he devastated as far as the cataracts of Syene (672). To his titles of king of Assyria and vicegerent of the gods he added that of king of Egypt and Ethiopia. A great number of Egyptians were transported to the banks of the Tigris. All the roads were covered with the unhappy captives, whom the conqueror, according to custom, drove before him like cattle.

Sardanapalus VI., a warrior not less terrible than his father, quenched in blood a revolt in Egypt. During his reign he had to struggle to maintain his authority throughout his vast empire, which he extended to the southern coast of Asia Minor. This was the last conquest of Assyria, now exhausted by its victories.

ASSOURDAN; RUIN OF NINIVE (625).—Phräortes, proclaimed king of Media, drove out the Assyrians and united Persia to his new kingdom. Believing himself powerful enough to overcome the Assyrians, he marched against the army of

King Assourdan as far as Ragan; but he lost both the battle and his life (635). His son, Cyaxeres, inherited his crown and his ambition. An invasion of Media by the Scythians soon taxed all the energies of the young monarch. No sooner had he repelled the barbarians than he lent his aid to Nabopolassar, governor of Babylon, to besiege Ninive.

Ninive, so long the mistress of Asia, was more than fifty miles in circuit. Even in the ninth century B.C., when the prophet Jonas preached penance there, many days were required to traverse the city. There were then in Ninive, according to the testimony of Holy Scriptures, more than one hundred and twenty thousand children not knowing their right hand from their left—a number that indicates a population of not less than two millions. The strength and beauty of Ninive corresponded to its greatness. It contained a great number of temples and magnificent palaces, built by its last kings. Its walls were one hundred feet in height, and so broad that on them three chariots could easily drive abreast. These walls were flanked with fifteen hundred towers, each not less than two hundred feet in height. All these means of defence, however, could not preserve Ninive from the rage of the Medes and the Babylonians. Assourdan slew himself in despair, and the conquerors, irritated by the long resistance of

Ninive, reduced that superb city to a mere heap of ruins.

God had announced by the prophets that he would revenge himself on Ninive for the blood of his people which she had shed, and that he would destroy her utterly, and there should remain no trace of the proud city. Indeed, the Greeks and the Romans were unable to recognize its site. The place where Ninive once existed was not known until about the year 1843, when M. Botta, French consul at Mosul, having excavated some of the vast mounds on the left bank of the Tigris, discovered there some ruins of the capital of the Assyrian Empire. These discoveries have been followed by those of Mr. Layard and other antiquarians.

Sec. 2. BABYLONIAN OR CHALDEAN EMPIRE (625–538 B.C.) : *Nabuchodonosor the Great (604–561 B.C.); Taking of Babylon by Cyrus (538 B.C.); Institutions and Customs of the Assyrians and Babylonians.*

PREPONDERANCE OF BABYLON ; NABOPOLASSAR (625–604).—In destroying the first Assyrian Empire (789), Phul had secured to Babylon a momentary preponderance which sustained his successor, Nabonassar, celebrated for having given his name to the era that began in 747, the year of his advent. But the rival of Ninive fell likewise under the Assyrian yoke. God, by the mouth of his prophets, had announced that he would give them back their power, that they might be an instrument of justice against Assyria and the kingdom of Juda. The Chaldean Nabopolassar, governor of Babylon, had accomplished the first part of this divine mission in the destruction of Ninive (625); he prepared the way to the fall of the kingdom of Juda by founding the Babylonian or Chaldean Empire, which stretched from the Tigris to the Mediterranean. Nechao, King of Egypt, desiring to have a part in the spoils of Ninive, occupied the country of the Philistines and Syria (610). The king of Babylon, now old and unable alone to avenge this injury, associated with himself his son Nabuchodonosor, whom he sent to combat the Egyptians on the Euphrates. The young prince defeated Nechao at Circesium, snatched his conquests from him, and even pursued him into Egypt; but, hearing of the death of his father, he hastened to return to Babylon.

NABUCHODONOSOR THE GREAT (604–561); RUIN OF THE KINGDOM OF JUDA (587).—The kingdom of Juda, placed between the Egyptians and the Babylonians, submitted by turns to the rival powers. After paying tribute to Nechao, the Israelites had everything to fear from the conqueror of Circesium. In fact, Nabuchodonosor threatening to besiege Jerusalem, King Joachim was constrained to pay him tribute and deliver to him hostages from the noblest families, among whom was the prophet Daniel, young, but already filled with wisdom (602). This was the beginning of that famous captivity of Babylon so often predicted by Jeremias.

The king and the people of Juda were humbled, but, still impenitent, continued by their bad conduct to provoke the anger of Heaven. An attempt to revolt brought Nabuchodonosor again to Jerusalem. He seized all the treasures of the Temple and the palace, and dethroned Jechonias, who had reigned but three months. The young king was carried a captive to Babylon, together with the prophet Ezechiel and a multitude of warriors and artisans. (599). Sedecias, ascending the throne of his nephew, refused to listen to Jeremias, who advised him to bear with patience the Babylonian yoke, since the fall of that city was fast approaching. The king of Juda preferred to trust with blind confidence in the support of his allies, the kings of Egypt, Tyre, Moab, and Idumea. Nabuchodonosor, irritated at this new revolt, and, moreover, executing the divine purpose of vengeance, showed no clemency. Jerusalem was taken after a siege of two years. Sedecias, the last king of Juda, had his eyes plucked out and was sent, loaded with chains, to Babylon, as were all those who had escaped the sword of the conqueror. The

---+---

walls of the city were razed to their foundations, and the Temple of Solomon, so often profaned, was reduced to ashes (587).

RUIN OF TYRE (574).—Nabuchodonosor, after having ravaged Lower Egypt, undertook the conquest of Phœnicia, whose riches he coveted. Even there he was the executor of the chastisement that God had announced by the mouth of Ezechiel: "For thus saith the Lord God: Behold, I will bring against Tyre Nabuchodonosor, King of Babylon, the king of kings, from the north, with horses, and chariots, and horsemen, and companies, and much people. . . . And he shall set engines of war and battering-rams against thy walls, and shall destroy thy towers with his arms. . . . And I will make thee like a naked rock; thou shalt be a drying-place for nets." The Tyrians made so obstinate a resistance that the siege lasted for thirteen years. Nabuchodonosor, having at last taken the city by assault, made the king and the principal inhabitants prisoners. In fulfilment of the prophecies he also, before returning to Babylon, devastated the countries of the Moabites and the Idumeans.

THE CITY OF BABYLON.—Nabuchodonosor, with the fruits of his conquests, raised in Babylon works so prodigious that that city passed among the ancients for the most beautiful city of the world. Two walls surrounded it with a double enclosure, one enclosing one hundred and

—✦—

twenty-eight square leagues, the other about seventy-two. .The great outer wall, more than two hundred feet high, was flanked with two hundred and fifty towers, and was defended by a large ditch filled with water, and by one hundred gates of massive brass. These two enclosures, which formed a parallelogram, contained highly-cultivated gardens and fields. The city occupied both banks of the Euphrates. On the left bank was the royal city—that which Nimrod had founded. Nabuchodonosor erected here a palace remarkable both for its size and magnificence. Here were the famous hanging gardens, which the Greeks numbered among the seven wonders of the world. They were like an artificial mountain, formed of terraces rising one above the other, and covered with trees, plants, and verdure. The king wished that his wife, daughter of Cyaxeres, should still have before her eyes the picturesque scenes of Media, her native country. A still more celebrated monument, and the most ancient in the world, is the Tower of Babel, which Nabuchodonosor caused to be rebuilt, with the inscription that men had built it after the Deluge, but had abandoned it because of the confusion of tongues.

The Euphrates, which was the chief ornament of Babylon, with its quays and bridges, served to defend the city by its artificial windings. On the left bank existed the profane city, peopled chiefly with captives. The Hebrews had here their judges and ancient customs. Here they assembled to console each other in their exile, to weep over the misfortunes of Sion, and to call down vengeance on their oppressors.

CHASTISEMENT AND PENITENCE OF NABUCHODONOSOR.—Nabuchodonosor saw in a dream a tree whose top reached to the sky, and whose branches spread over the whole earth. At the same time he heard a voice saying: "Cut down the tree and lop off its branches, that it may be deprived of its heart of a man, and have the heart of a beast for seven years." The king, terrified, had recourse to Daniel, whom he found among the captives at Babylon. The holy prophet declared to the king that his dream would be accomplished in his own person, and that he would be reduced to the condition of a beast; Daniel also exhorted him to penitence for his wickedness.

The prediction was verified. One day, as the king, inflated with pride, was contemplating from his palace the city of Babylon, "Is not this," he cried, "that great Babylon which I myself have built in all the splendor of my glory?" That same instant he lost his reason; was driven from the company of men and became as the beasts, exposed to the inclemency of the weather, and ate of the grass of the fields. After the appointed time had expired his reason was restored;

he acknowledged the greatness of God, and pro-foundly humbled himself in the presence of him who is the sovereign arbiter of kings as well as of people. God, satisfied with his penitence, gave him back his human form. He reascended the throne and became more powerful than ever. Penetrated with gratitude, Nabuchodonosor pub-lished a solemn edict proclaiming the marvels God had wrought in his behalf. He died a year after (561 B.C.), and, we have every reason to be-lieve, in sentiments of true piety. He was one of the greatest monarchs that ever reigned in Asia.

TAKING OF BABYLON BY CYRUS (538).—The empire of Nabuchodonosor, weakened by the vices of his unworthy successors,* found itself threatened by a formidable enemy. Cyrus, at the head of the Medes and Persians, advanced against Babylon. The siege of that place was not an easy enterprise. The city was of vast ex-tent, well fortified, supplied with provisions for many years, and contained an immense number

---

* The successors of Nabuchodonosor were : Evil-merodach (561-559), his son, a pacific prince, but weak, who knew the true God and honored the prophet Daniel with his favor without renouncing the worship of idols ; Neriglissar (559-555), brother-in-law of Evil-mero-dach, and his murderer, perished in a battle against the Persians ; Laboroso-archod (555), son of Neriglissar, dethroned on account ot his cruelty ; Nabonadas (555-538), named king by the Chaldeans, and de-feated by Cyrus near Babylon ; Balthassar, associated to the throne by his father Nabonadas and charged to defend Babylon ; but this prince joined to indolence the two vices which have ever preceded the fall of empires, licentiousness and impiety.

of inhabitants determined to defend it. The besieged insulted Cyrus and his army from the top
of the walls. Unheeding their taunts, Cyrus
caused a large and deep canal to be dug in
order to turn off the Euphrates, which was the
chief defence of Babylon. Hardly was the work
accomplished when he learned that the Babylonians were going to celebrate a feast at which
they were accustomed to pass the entire night in
feasting and debauchery. The occasion was
deemed favorable by Cyrus for taking the city.
To this end, early in the night he ordered the
communication between the river and the canal
to be opened; the waters rushed into the latter
precipitately, and soon left the bed of the river
dry. By this channel the Persians entered the
city. The impious king Balthassar had that very
night profaned the sacred vessels of the Temple
of Jerusalem, and he was slain by the victors,
who were but the instruments of divine vengeance. It is worthy of remark that the prophet
Isaias had predicted that the Persians and the
Medes would break the pride of Babylon, and
had called Cyrus himself by name more than
one hundred years before his birth.

Babylon, after many useless revolts, was gra-
dually deserted, until finally it was little more
than a heap of ruins. All travellers agree in
saying that the prophecy was literally fulfilled: "Babylon, glorious among kingdoms,

the famous pride of the Chaldeans, shall be even as the Lord destroyed Sodom and Gomorrha. It shall no more be inhabited for ever, and it shall not be founded unto generation and generation : neither shall the Arabian pitch his tents there, nor shall shepherds rest there. But wild beasts shall rest there, and their houses shall be filled with serpents, and ostriches shall dwell there, and the hairy ones shall dance there: and owls shall answer one another there, in the houses thereof, and sirens in the temples of pleasure."

Sec. 3. RELIGION; *Government; Sciences; Arts; Cuneiform Writing.*

RELIGION.—The Assyrians and Babylonians, although early falling into idolatry, nevertheless preserved some notion of one Supreme Being, which some thought to be Assur, the founder of Ninive, and others to be Bel or Baal, who appears the same as Nimrod, the founder of Babylon. With these two principal divinities were often associated Merodach, the great lord, "who confides to the king the government of nations," and Nebo, or the "supreme intelligence." The sun, moon, and the other planets were still objects of particular worship, especially among the Chaldeans, who attributed to the stars a great influence over human affairs. The people were believers in the grossest polytheism. We learn from the Bible that at the period when the

Assyrian colonies occupied the kingdom of Israel "each one made his god in the city in which he dwelt."

GOVERNMENT.—The kings of Ninive and Babylon assumed the title of "vicegerents of the gods over the earth " They did not claim, like the kings of Egypt, to be gods themselves, though their authority was not less absolute or less respected by their subjects. When they appeared in public the insignia of their authority were the same as those yet seen in Asia—the parasol and large fly-flap of plumes carried by slaves. The court of the monarch was composed of his ministers, and a great number of officers charged with superintending the place and the administration of affairs. Among the provinces of the empire some were simple vassals or tributaries, and preserved their own form of government; the others, incorporated with the empire, had their satraps, or prefects, for governors. If we except the Chaldeans, they had no castes or privileged classes. The most important functions were often entrusted to strangers, as we see in the history of Daniel. The Babylonians and the Assyrians, who were of a practical turn of mind, observed the greatest exactness in the measurement of their lands and the imposition of taxes. Each Babylonian had a staff on which were inscribed his name, that of his father, and that of the god he had chosen for his patron. To this was added some distinctive sign or personal symbol, which was a kind of escutcheon. The women, on the day of their marriage, received an olive of baked clay, which they wore on the neck, and on which were inscribed their name, that of their husband, and the date of their marriage.

SCIENCES.—The sciences most successfully cultivated were mathematics and astronomy. By a skilful system of decimal and duodecimal numeration the unit was divided into sixty equal parts, which were subdivided in the same manner. The Babylonians were the first to divide the day into twenty-four hours, the hour into sixty minutes, and the minute into sixty seconds. It is thought that Pythagoras borrowed from them the famous multiplication-table which bears his name. Attentive observers of the stars under a serene sky, they made sufficient progress in astronomy to ascertain the lunar and solar year; they were even able to predict the eclipses of the moon, but their science was too imperfect to predict those of the sun. Astrology was in honor among the Chaldeans, who, by means of the stars, announced beforehand, ordinarily in almanacs, the secrets of the future. Magic to them was not less useful, since they believed it able to cure all maladies. The profession of medicine was unknown. The sick, when they had not recourse to magicians, asked advice of every one they met. If they were not able to walk, they

——❖——

were carried to the highway, and the passers-by were invited to give their opinion on the most efficacious treatment and remedy. This custom contrasted with that of Egypt, where every kind of sickness had its appointed physician.

ARTS; CUNEIFORM WRITING.—The distinctive character of the Assyrian monuments is the grandeur of their proportions joined to the richness of their decorations, which consisted of statues, bas-reliefs, and paintings in fresco. They raised at first considerable mounds or artificial columns, on which they built temples, palaces, or even cities. All their buildings were of brick, either baked or merely dried in the sun. They embellished the bricks by means of an enamel discovered by the Babylonians. Besides the art of enamelling, the Babylonians and the Assyrians possessed the secret of making with rare perfection furniture, jewels, carved arms, tissues of wool, and linen robes and carpets ornamented with embroidery and vivid coloring.

But the most difficult art, and the most in honor, was the cuneiform writing. This writing is so called from the form of the characters, which resembles a wedge. These characters were traced with a triangular stiletto on tablets of soft clay, which were baked when they wished to preserve them. In a library recently discovered at Ninive each book was composed of a series of these tablets, which are numbered as well as the leaves of the same work. A great number of cuneiform inscriptions are graven on the bricks and stones. They read from right to left. It was not till our times that this complicated system of writing was deciphered, and this valuable discovery has resulted in confirming and explaining many passages in Holy Scriptures.

REVIEW QUESTIONS.

By whom was Babylon built? Ninive? Who was Nimrod? Assur? Where was Abram born? (What of him?) When and by whom were Babylon and Ninive reduced to vassalage? Who founded the first Assyrian Empire? What of Tiglath-pileser? What did the Lord say of Assyria? Who was the instrument of his vengeance? Describe Sardanapalus III.? What of his son? What can you say of Semiramis?) Why did Arbaces revolt? How did Sardanapalus V. live? Describe the manner of his death? (What cruel policy did Tiglath-pileser II. introduce? Describe the taking of Samaria? What was the fate of Sargon? How was the impious Sennacherib punished? In what words did Isaias prophesy his destruction? By whom was Manasses made captive? What was the last conquest of Assyria?) Describe the city of Ninive? When and by whom was its site discovered? Why did God give back its power to Babylon? By whom was the kingdom of Juda conquered in 587 B.C.? Describe the captivity of Babylon? What did Ezechiel say of Tyre? How long did the siege last? Describe the city of Babylon? Its hanging gardens? The Euphrates? What chastisement was inflicted on Nabuchodonosor, and why? In what way did Cyrus take the city of Babylon? What prophecy did its utter ruin literally fulfil? What was the religion of the Assyrians and Babylonians? What form of government prevailed amongst them? In the knowledge of what sciences were they most advanced? How did their treatment of the sick differ from that of the Egyptians? In what arts did they excel? Describe their system of writing.

CHAPTER III.

MEDIA AND PERSIA.

THE history of Media and Persia is divided into two periods: 1. From the remotest times to the death of Cyrus (529 B.C.) 2. From the death of Cyrus to the beginning of the Median wars (529–500 B.C.)

Sec. 1. ORIGIN OF THE MEDES AND PER-SIANS; *Government of the Medes before Cyrus* (650–559 B.C.) ; *Conquest and Empire of Cyrus* (559–529 B.C.)

ORIGIN OF THE MEDES ; DEJOCES (710–657).—While the descendants of Cham and of Sem were founding Babylon and Ninive the descendants of Japheth, who called themselves the Aryans—that is, "the noble" or "excellent"—occupied Bactriana and the neighboring countries. Some, directing their course towards the northwest, peopled Egypt ; others went either to the south of India, or to the southwest, to Media and Persia.

The Medes, so called from Madai, son of Japheth, appear' to have formed the two principal classes—that of the *Magi*, or "great," and that of warriors. It is thought that the first inhabitants of the country subjugated by the Medes, properly so called, formed the four inferior classes of agriculturists, shepherds, serfs, and nomads. It is certain that Media became in the tenth century a tributary province of the first Assyrian Empire. Arbaces restored its independence when he destroyed that empire (789), but he left it divided into several tribes, who would neither dwell in peace nor defend their country against the conquering monarchs of the second Assyrian Empire.

At last the Medes, wearied of anarchy, chose for king Dejoces (710), who was noted for his wisdom and equity. The new prince re-established order and built Ecbatana, capital of Media. This city, situated on an isolated hill, had seven enclosures, which rose like an amphitheatrè. The inner enclosed the palace and the treasures of the king; the six others were inhabited by the people, who were not able to penetrate to the palace; there were even severe penalties inflicted on whoever looked upon the monarch, or laughed or expectorated in his presence. √

SUBMISSION OF PERSIA (650); CONQUESTS OF PHRAORTES (657–635) AND OF CYAXARES I. (635–595).—The Persians, as also the Medes, their neighbors, were descended from Japheth. They were divided into three classes: warriors, agriculturists, and nomads. These three classes comprised ten tribes, which were leagued together under the government of a chief chosen from the first tribe of warriors, called Pasargados. Achemenes governed Persia in the middle of the seventh century, and was attacked by Phraortes, son and successor of Dejoces. He could make but little resistance, and acknowledged himself vassal of the king of Media.

Phraortes, pursuing his conquests, also subjugated Parthia, Bactriana, and all Central Asia. Armenia, even, had acknowledged him as sovereign, when he lost his life, as we have elsewhere seen, in a battle against the king of Ninive (635). Cyaxares I., his son and successor, hastened to avenge him by destroying the second Assyrian Empire (625), thus extending his kingdom from the left bank of the Tigris to the interior of Armenia, where he had soon to combat the Lydians.

The Lydians, descendants of Lud, son of Sem, had become the most powerful people in Asia Minor. Already masters of Troy and several other cities of Ionia, they also conquered Phrygia and Cappadocia. Their king, named Alyattes (614–558), feared not to offer protection to a vassal tribe of Cyaxares, King of the Medes. This was the cause of a long and desperate war, which ended at the battle of the "Eclipse," so-called because an eclipse of the sun, suddenly changing the day into night, so terrified the combat-

-- ✦ ---

ants that they threw down their arms and concluded peace (5u5); the king of Lydia ceding
that part of Cappadocia situated on the right
bank of the Halys, and giving his daughter in
marriage to Astyages, son of Cyaxares I. √

ASTYAGES (595–559); WISDOM OF THE YOUNG
CYRUS.—Astyages, less enterprising than his two
predecessors, contented himself with governing
in peace his vast empire. To secure the fidelity
of the Persians, he gave his daughter's hand to
Cambyses, grandson of Achemenes. Of this
marriage was born Cyrus, one of the most famous conquerors of Asia.

Cyrus was reared according to the laws of the
country, which, for those times, were excellent
with respect to education. From his infancy he
appeared full of sweetness and sincerity. This
disposition, joined to great docility, soon rendered him superior to all other children of his
age.

When Cyrus had reached the age of twelve,
his mother took him with her to Media, to his
grandfather, Astyages. Cyrus was not dazzled
by the pomp and pride of the court, but retained
all his virtuous principles. Astyages, who
wished him to give up the desire to return to
Persia, one day prepared a sumptuous banquet.
Cyrus regarded the preparations with much in-
difference. "The Persians," said he to the
king, "instead of going such a roundabout way

——✠——

to appease their hunger, have a much shorter and easier method: a little bread and some cresses answer their purpose."

After a sojourn of four years at the court of Media Cyrus returned to Persia, where the lessons and examples of his father soon perfected him in the art of government and in military science.

Cyrus (559–529) and Cyaxares II. (559–536); Campaign against the Assyrians (555). —On the death of Astyages (559), if we credit Xenophon, the crown of Media passed to his son Cyaxares.* The latter having asked aid against the Assyrians, Cyrus marched to his relief with thirty thousand chosen men. Cambyses accompanied his son to the frontiers of Persia, and on the way gave him excellent instructions concerning the duties of a general. One day the question was discussed how to make soldiers obedient and submissive. "The means," said Cyrus,

* Xenophon is the only historian who speaks of Cyaxares II., son and successor of Astyages. Herodotus and others assert that Astyages had no other child than Mandana, the wife of Cambyses, and that he wished to kill his grandson because he had been warned in a dream that Cyrus would deprive him of his kingdom. But Cyrus was saved by one of the king's shepherds and reared as his son till the age of ten years. The nobleness of his character betrayed his origin. Recognized by his grandfather, he was sent into Persia. Having there aided his countrymen to throw off the yoke of Media, he placed himself at their head and defeated two armies, one commanded by his grandfather. Astyages was made prisoner, and Cyrus became sole king of the Medes and Persians (559). This account of Herodotus is now preferred, not as being certain, but as being more plausible than that of Xenophon.

—✠—

" seem to me very easy: it is only to praise and reward those who obey, and to punish and degrade those who do not." "That is the way," replied Cambyses, " to make them obey by force; but the chief point is how to make them obey willingly. Now, the sure method of doing this is to convince those you command that you are more skilful and prudent than they." "But what must one do," said Cyrus, "to appear more skilful and prudent than others?" "He must really be so," replied Cambyses; " and, in order to be so, he must apply himself closely to his profession, diligently study all its rules, consult with docility the most able masters, and, above all, he must implore the assistance of Heaven, which alone bestows wisdom and success."

When Cyrus arrived in Media he distinguished himself not only by the luxury of his table and his equipage, but also by his justice and generosity, which gained the affection of all his troops. The young prince, seeing them full of ardor, proposed to lead them against the Assyrians and to invade the enemy's country. The Assyrians came out to meet them. But the Medes and Persians, animated by the presence and example of Cyrus, repulsed them with such vigor that the enemy were utterly routed. The vanquished were pursued to their camp, and a terrible slaughter ensued, in which the Assyrian king perished.

MARRIAGE OF CYRUS.—After many conquests

resulting from this victory, Cyrus, desirous to return to Media, announced his arrival to Cyaxares, who was on the frontier with reserved troops. This prince, jealous of the glory of his nephew, and fearing that he might entertain ambitious designs, received him coldly and turned his face from his embrace. Cyrus, whose prudence equalled his valor, entered into an explanation with his uncle. He spoke to him with so much mildness and submission that he dispelled all Cyaxares' suspicions and completely regained his favor.

Cyaxares, more charmed than ever with the good qualities of Cyrus, offered him his only daughter in marriage, with Media for her dowry; for he was himself the sole heir of that crown at the death of Astyages. Cyrus, though grateful for so advantageous a proposal, would not accept it till he had obtained the consent of his father and mother, leaving an admirable example to all future ages of the respectful deference which children, whatever be their age or their qualifications, should pay to their parents. He made a journey to Persia, from which he had been absent six years; on his return he married the princess, and thus became heir to the throne of Media.*

WAR AGAINST CRŒSUS; BATTLE OF THYMBRA

* Thus, according to Xenophon, Cyrus could not have been king of the Medes and Persians until the death of Cyaxeres (536).

(544).—About the middle of the fourth century B.C. there were four great powers in the East—Media, the Babylonian Empire, Lydia, and Egypt. Cyrus, destined to replace them by Persian rule, was already marshalling the forces of Media when he was called to meet Crœsus, King of Lydia, who had formed a formidable league with the kings of Egypt and Babylon.

This monarch had just subjugated nearly all of Asia Minor, but he was still more celebrated for his immense riches. Some even assert that he was the first to coin gold. Uneasy at seeing Cyrus extend his conquests to the foot of the Caucasus, he sent to consult the oracle of Delphi, and received the response that, if he undertook the war, he would destroy a great empire. Full of confidence in the oracle, he crossed the Halys with his troops and those of his allies; but at the end of an indecisive campaign he judged it prudent to retreat towards Thymbra.

Near that city Cyrus, with two hundred thousand men and three hundred war-chariots armed with scythes, offered battle to the enemy. Crœsus, who did not lack courage, and whose troops were twice as numerous as those of his enemy, accepted the challenge. He ranged his army in a single line, three leagues in length. Cyrus disposed his troops with more skill. He formed three lines, the first of soldiers heavily armed, the second of lancers, the third of archers, who could cast their darts from behind the other two lines, and who were' thus shielded by a double rampart. Then, invoking in a loud voice the God of his fathers, he mounted his horse and marched against the enemy. His war-chariots at once threw them into disorder; the combat was not very obstinate, and, after a feeble resistance, the allies were routed and put to flight.

CAPTIVITY OF CRŒSUS; CONQUEST OF ASIA MINOR.—Cyrus, the day after the battle, marched towards Sardis, the capital of Lydia. Having defeated Crœsus a second time, he besieged that city, which yielded in a few days. Crœsus himself fell into the hands of the Persians.* Cyrus, touched by the misfortune of a king who had been regarded as the most fortunate of mortals, treated him with clemency and kindness. He

---

* Herodotus relates that after the capture of Sardis Crœsus was on the point of being slain by a soldier who did not know him. His son, who had been mute from birth, was greatly terrified, and, making a great effort, cried out: "Soldier, do not slay Crœsus!" His filial piety was rewarded by the gift of speech. Later on, Crœsus, loaded with chains, was about to perish on a funeral pile, when he was heard to repeat the name of Solon. When asked his reason, he declared that the Athenian legislator, on beholding his immense riches, had said to him that no one could esteem himself happy while he lived. Cyrus, reflecting on the uncertainty of earthly things, was fain to pardon his captive. The latter, carrying his chains to Delphi, reproached the god for having deceived him. The oracle replied that, according to the prophecy, Crœsus, having undertaken the war, had destroyed a great empire; but that Crœsus deceived himself in undertaking a war without asking which great empire he would destroy, his own or that of the Persians.

—•—

wished to have him always near his person, and asked his advice on the most important affairs.

The conquest of Lydia entailed that of the whole of Asia Minor. Most of the cities of Ionia would not yield till after a sharp struggle. The Phocians, rather than submit to the Persian yoke, embarked with their families and sought refuge in Marseilles, founded by their ancestors.

CAPTURE OF BABYLON (538); EDICT OF CYRUS IN FAVOR OF THE JEWS (536).—Cyrus, having deprived the King of Babylon of all his allies, went to besiege him in his capital. We have already seen how he took this great city and destroyed the Babylonian or Chaldean Empire, which had lasted eighty-seven years (625–538).

Cyrus, master of Babylon, was flattered to learn that the prophets of Juda had a long time before announced his triumph. His first care was to put an end to the captivity of the Jews, who had languished under a stranger's rule for seventy years. He published an edict in which he declared that, the Lord God of Israel having given him all the kingdoms of the earth, it was his duty to erect a temple to his honor in Jerusalem. He therefore invited all the Jews to return to their country, and promised to protect them against whoever attempted to thwart the re-establishment of the Temple of God.

END OF THE REIGN OF CYRUS.—Cyrus, beloved by his subjects, enjoyed in peace the fruit of his conquests. His empire, which had Ecbatana for its capital, extended from the Indus to the Ægean Sea, from the Indian Ocean to the Caspian and Euxine Seas.

This great monarch preserved to the last a strong and robust constitution, which was the recompense of the sober and frugal life he had always led. He died, aged seventy years, with the reputation of the wisest conqueror and the most accomplished prince that had yet reigned. Happily disabused of the senseless worship of idols and brought by the prophet Daniel to the knowledge of the true God, he had had the courage to serve and glorify the Creator of heaven and earth and the Sovereign Master of peoples and kings.*

Sec. 2. CAMBYSES (529–522 B.C.); *the False Smerdis* (522–521 B.C.); *Darius I. before the Median Wars* (521–500 B.C.); *Institutions and Customs of the Medes and Persians.*

CAMBYSES (529–522); CONQUEST OF EGYPT (525); REPULSE IN ETHIOPIA.—Cambyses, eldest

---

* Herodotus differs from Xenophon concerning the death as well as the childhood of Cyrus. Cyrus, according to the former, terminated his reign in a war against the Massagetes. Having defeated these barbarians and slain the son of their queen, Tomyris, he fell into an ambuscade, in which he lost two hundred thousand men and was made prisoner. Tomyris, having cut off his head, put it in a cask filled with blood, saying: "Glut thyself with blood after thy death, since thou wert so insatiable for it during thy life."

son of Cyrus, inherited his throne, but not his virtues. We have seen how he conquered Egypt. This was followed by the submission of Libya and Cyrenaica. Inflated by his success, the conqueror wished to subjugate Ethiopia. He set out without provisions; but his temerity cost him more than half his army, which died of famine or was buried in the sand. Returning to Memphis, he found it in a tumult of rejoicing. Imagining that they rejoiced because of his ill-success, he caused all the magistrates to be slain; but learning that it was because they had found their god Apis, he commanded it to be brought to him, that he might, he said, make its acquaintance. But the prince was greatly astonished when, instead of a god, he saw an ox. Transported with fury, he stabbed it with his dagger.

FURIOUS PASSION OF CAMBYSES.—Cambyses, whose disposition daily became more ferocious, killed his brother Smerdis on bare suspicion, having no other foundation than a dream. His sister having wept over this loss, the furious prince killed her with a kick. This rendered him so odious that a magician named Smerdis, strikingly resembling the prince of that name, caused himself to be proclaimed king as the true son and successor of Cyrus. Cambyses, enraged at this, marched against the usurper; but as he mounted his horse his sword slipped from its scabbard, inflicting a wound of which he died (522),

---

CONSPIRACY AGAINST THE MAGICIAN SMER-
DIS.—The death of Cambyses secured the crown
for a time to the false Smerdis. He endeavored
to conceal his imposture, but his very precautions
caused him to be suspected. Through a confi-
dential attendant, who lived in the palace, the
Persians learned that the man who now reigned
over them had formerly had his ears cut off by
order of Cyrus. Upon the verification of this
fact the nobles resolved to deliver their country·
and themselves from the usurper. Darius, son
of Hystaspes, and six other nobles formed a conspiracy, and, entering the palace, killed the false
Smerdis and showed his head to the people, that
the imposture might be publicly known. The
people, in their fury, massacred the greater number of the magicians, who had been the most
zealous partisans of the usurper.

DARIUS I. (521–485); TAKING OF BABYLON
(518).—The conspirators proclaimed Darius
king. He belonged to the illustrious family of
Achemenides.* From the outset of his reign he

---

* The murderers of the impostor Smerdis, according to Herodotus,
had agreed that on the following morning they would depart from
the city, and would acknowledge him king whose horse should be
the first to greet with his neighing the rising sun. The groom of Darius, having concealed his mare near where the pretenders passed,
thus secured to his master the crown. The latter, it is said, left an
inscription attesting that he owed the crown to his charioteer and
horse. It is certain that Darius did not speak of this in a cuneiform
inscription where he gave an account of the first events of his reign.
This inscription, but lately deciphered, was found on a structure
of Bisoutoun, in Persia.

had to suppress many revolts in the tributary countries. The most formidable was that of the Babylonians, the bitter enemies of the Medes and Persians. Darius came to attack them with all his forces. In order to make their provisions last the longer, they barbarously destroyed all useless consumers. Darius, after twenty months of siege, began to despair of success, when a novel stratagem opened to him the gates of the city.

One of the noblemen of his court, Zopyrus, appeared one day before him covered with blood, his nose and ears cut off. At this spectacle the king cried out: " Who has thus treated you ? " " Yourself," replied Zopyrus. " My desire to render you service has reduced me to this condition. I am going to join your enemies, and may thus enable you to conquer them." With much concern Darius saw him depart. Zopyrus approached the city, where he was well known, and was permitted to enter. Then he told them of his misfortune, and the cruel treatment he had received for having endeavored to persuade the king to raise the siege.

The Babylonians believed him and placed him at the head of some troops, with which he achieved signal successes over the besiegers; thenceforth he was thought to be the implacable enemy of Darius, and was made general of the Babylonian forces. Darius approaching the walls at a time agreed upon, the gates were opened, and thus the Persians became masters of a city which neither famine nor force could subdue. The king recompensed Zopyrus by making him governor of Babylon. About this time Darius, learning of the edict of Cyrus in favor of the Jews, also granted them his protection and money to rebuild the temple of Jerusalem, which Zorobabel solemnly dedicated (515).

EXPEDITION AGAINST THE SCYTHIANS (508–506).—Cyrus had conquered Asia, and Cambyses Egypt. Darius, who aspired to equal his predecessors, determined to conquer Europe. He first turned his arms against the Scythians, who had lately ravaged Asia Minor. These people occupied the country between the Danube and Tanaïs.

They lived in great innocence and simplicity. Milk and honey were their chief diet, while they defended themselves from the rigor of the climate with the skins of wild beasts. Gold and silver were not current among them. Justice was administered through choice, and not from fear of law, of which they knew nothing. Without arts or sciences, they possessed more wisdom than the Greeks, notwithstanding their philosophers and lawgivers. Such is the picture that profane writers, and especially poets, present us of Scythia.

It was against this people that Darius first declared war. He departed from Susa with an army of six hundred thousand men, marched towards the Thracian Bosporus, which he crossed, as also the Danube, on a bridge of boats. At his approach the Scythians filled up their wells and destroyed all the forage in those parts through which the Persian army was to pass. They then retreated before the Persians, to draw them into the interior of the country. Darius had the imprudence to persist in his rash enterprise, and his army soon suffered from famine. He sent a herald to the Scythian king with this message : " Prince of the Scythians, wherefore dost thou fly before me ? Why not stop and give me battle, if thou canst resist me ; or submit, if thou art weaker than I ?" The Scythians mocked Darius and continued to retreat.

When the Persian army was reduced to the last extremity, the Scythians sent a herald, who was commissioned to present to Darius a bird, a mouse, a frog, and five arrows. Darius thought at first that these presents were a token of submission on the part of the Scythians, but one of his officers gave them a different meaning. " Know," said he to the Persians, " that unless you can fly in the air like birds, or hide yourself in the earth like mice, or dive under the water like frogs, you shall not escape the arrows of the Scythians."

In fact, the Persians, finding famine awaiting them, thought only of retreating. It was not, however, without great difficulty and danger that

———⁖———

Darius, covered with shame, led the remnants of his troops to the Danube, which he hastened to place between him and his enemy. To efface the disgrace of this imprudent expedition he left in Europe his lieutenant, Megabyzus, who, with eighty thousand men, imposed tribute on Mace donia, subjugated Thrace, and occupied Byzan tium, on the Bosporus.

EMPIRE OF THE PERSIANS UNDER DARIUS.— At the time when Darius engaged in the war against the Greeks his empire extended to Eu rope, and comprised, in Africa, Egypt, with Libya and Cyrenaica, and, in Asia, all the coun‑ tries beyond the Indus and Jaxartes. There had never before been so vast an empire. It was in the central city of Susa that Darius fixed his residence. This capital and the city of Persepo‑ lis, destined to serve as the royal burial-place, were adorned with magnificent marble palaces. Darius, to meet these expenses, divided his empire into twenty satrapies and fixed the tax that each had to pay. This measure, in which he showed rare moderation, rendered him odious to his subjects. The Persians, who had called Cyrus's father, Cambyses, Master, could find no other surname for Darius than Merchant, because he made money of everything.

RELIGION.—The religion of the Persians was that which Zoroaster had taught. He was a legislator and conqueror who lived about the year

2000 B.C. It is related that he attempted to restore the primitive faith by substituting for idolatry the worship of one perfect, eternal God, who created all things, and who governed them with the assistance of good spirits. But Zoroaster, not being able to account for the existence of sin, attributed it to an evil God, assisted by evil spirits. Hence arose a desperate conflict between the two gods—*Ahriman*, the author of evil, and *Ormuzd*, the author of good, represented by light, fire, and the sun—above all, the rising sun.

This conflict was destined to terminate at the end of the world by the intervention of a god greater than Ormuzd or Ahriman. The latter, with his followers, would be cast into an eternal prison; the former be rewarded, with his disciples, by the enjoyment of eternal happiness. Hence the Persians admitted the immortality of the soul, with the rewards and punishments of an after-life. The bodies of their dead were buried in place of being embalmed, like the Egyptians, or burned, like the Romans. Their priests were termed *magi;* they had among them what the Gauls called Druids—that is, the wise, the learned, and the philosophers of Persia.

GOVERNMENT.—The Persian monarch enjoyed boundless power; he was called "the great king," "the king of kings." His palace was called the "Gate" (so called yet among the

——✦——

Turks). ' A severe etiquette forbade all entrance.'
A crowd of officers were stationed, according to
their rank, in the outer courts to serve as media-
tors between the king and subject; they were
called "the eyes and ears of the king."

, A council of ministers was charged with the
most important affairs. Each satrapy was gov-,
erned by a satrap with unlimited powers. Deposed,
at will, he sought but to enrich himself at the expense of his province ; hence the luxury and des-,
potism of the satraps passed into a proverb among,
the Greeks. It was under Darius I. that the
love of riches began to enervate the Persians.
Xenophon, who lived within a century after that,
monarch, acknowledged that the manners of the
Persians no longer corresponded to the brilliant
picture he drew of them in his *Cyropedia.*

. ORDER OF BATTLE AND ATTACK.—The Persians were very warlike before the time of Cyrus,
but this prince carried the military science to a,
far higher degree of perfection than any previous,
conqueror. The celebrated battle of Thymbra
may give us an idea of his manner of arranging
the troops. The infantry were placed in the
centre, their two wings covered by the cavalry,
which gave them more liberty to act. The army
was arranged in several lines, each sustaining the
other.

. The first line was of infantry ranged twelve
men deep, armed with partisans, swords, and

———✠———

battle-axes. Behind these lightly-armed soldiers were placed, who flung their javelins over
the heads of the first line. The archers and spear-
men formed the third line. Lastly came the
rolling towers, each defended by fifteen or twenty
men. These towers served to rally the troops in
case they were broken and pushed by the enemy.
Chariots armed with scythes were also used;
these were usually placed in the front, or as a
guard for the wings.

The first method of attacking a city was by
blockade. It was invested with a wall, or
else a deep trench was dug around it, fenced
with palisades, to hinder the besieged from
making a sally, and to prevent succor or provisions from being brought in. The second
method was by scaling; but as the walls of
the cities were often higher than the lad-
ders, moving towers of wood were built, which,
being higher than the walls, gave easy admittance
into the besieged city. The third method was
the battering-ram. This was a vast beam of
timber with a strong head of iron or brass at its
end, which was impelled with great force against
the walls, making a breach which formed a passage for the soldiers. The fourth method was
that of sapping or mining, and this was done in
two different ways—either by carrying a subterranean path under the city and thus affording
access, or, after sapping the walls and putting

supporters under it, filling the spaces with combustible matter and setting it on fire, thus throwing down the walls. The two last-named methods were not used till after the time of Cyrus.

REVIEW QUESTIONS.

Who were the Aryans? Where did they settle? Into how many classes were the Medes divided? Name the superior classes. The inferior. What of Arbaces? Dejoces? Describe Ecbatana. From whom were the Persians descended? How were they classed? By whom was Persia conquered? What of him? His son? Who were the Lydians? By whom, ere they attacked, and why? What brought the war to a close? Who was Cyrus? What can you say of his childhood? Describe his visit to his grandfather. What advice did his father give him? What course did Cyrus pursue in Media? What followed? How did he obtain the daughter of Cyaxares in marriage? Who was Crœsus? What made him so famous? Describe the battle of Thymbra. How did Cyrus treat the captive king? What does Herodotus say? Having taken Babylon, what edict did Cyrus publish? What did he promise to the Jews? How far did the empire of Cyrus extend? Describe his death according to Xenophon. According to Herodotus. Why did not Cambyses subdue Ethiopia. On his return to Memphis what occurred? What was the character of Cambyses? How did he end his life? By whom was he succeeded? What became of the false Smerdis? How did Darius gain possession of Babylon? What privilege did he grant to the Jews? Where did the Scythians live? Describe their character. Why did Darius invade Scythia? How did the Scythians baffle him? What message did the Persian herald bear? The Scythian herald? How did the expedition terminate? What was the extent of the Persian empire under Darius? What rendered him odious to his subjects? What form of religion prevailed in Persia? Who were the magi? How was the Persian king styled? His palace? What was meant by "the ears and eyes of the king"? Who were the satraps? Describe the Persian order of battle. Their four methods of attacking cities.

CHAPTER IV.

PHŒNICIA AND CARTHAGE.

THE history of Phœnicia blends first with Sidon and Tyre, then with that of Carthage.

Sec. 1. SIDON AND TYRE: *Commerce, Colonies, Industry, and Religion of the Phœnicians.*

SIDON AND TYRE.—The Phœnicians, descendants of Chanaan, son of Cham, occupied from early times the coast between the Mediterranean Sea and the southern line of Lebanon. Finding their continent too narrow, they turned their energies to the sea, and were the first to brave the dangers of navigation. Sidon, called "the city of fishermen" and "the eldest daughter of Chanaan," had already a flourishing commerce in the time of Abraham.

But the Phœnicians, while extending their power on the sea, remained too weak in their country not to fear the neighboring nations; they therefore became tributaries of Egypt in the seventeenth century B.C. They were equally powerless either to defend their brethren, the Chanaanites, from the Hebrews commanded by Josue, or to repel the attacks of the Philistines.

A Philistine fleet unexpectedly entered the port of Sidon and utterly destroyed the great Phœnician city (1209 B.C.).

Tyre inherited the power of Sidon, and obtained the supremacy over the other cities of Phœnicia. Holy Scripture tells us that their kings were ever the allies of the Jewish people. Hiram furnished Solomon with the workmen and materials necessary for constructing the Temple. Less than a century later, the impious Jezabel, a Tyrian princess, induced her consort, Achab, King of Israel, to renounce the worship of the true God.

The Jews, as well as the Phœnicians, met the chastisement due their crimes at the hands of the Assyrians. Tyre, that opulent city, whose destruction as well as prosperity had been announced by the prophets, was taken and destroyed by Nabuchodonosor the Great (574 B.C.). Her fall so terrified her colonies that Carthage and other states hastened to recognize the supremacy of the Babylonian Empire.

COMMERCE AND COLONIES.—The Phœnicians, having discovered the art of navigation, were the first to engage in maritime commerce. In order to exchange the products of their industry for those of the countries which they visited, they established marts, which soon became so many flourishing colonies. Thus they established themselves in Cyprus, Rhodes, and many other islands of the Ægean Sea, and on the shores of the Euxine.) Their vessels also ploughed the Mediterranean, and even ventured as far as the isles of Great Britain. (In these distant voyages the Phœnicians spread abroad the knowledge of useful arts, and the natives commemorated their pacific exploits in the celebrated legend of the Tyrian Hercules.)

Their principal colonies were, in Africa, Utica and Carthage; in Sicily, Selinontus and Panormus; in Spain, Malaga, Cadiz, and Seville. Their establishments were numerous in the rich country known under the name of Betica, supposed to be the *Tharsis* of the Bible. "Spain," says Ezechiel, "makes commerce with thee because of thy riches; she pays for thy products with silver, iron, tin, and lead." When the Phœnicians landed in Spain silver was so plentiful there that common utensils were made of that metal, and even the anchors of vessels.

The Phœnicians also carried on a land commerce hardly less active than that on sea. (This commerce extended all over Asia—to the north, by Armenia and the Caucasus; to the east, by Babylon; to the south, by Arabia.) Tyrian vessels went in search of the treasures of *Ophir*, a name which designates, according to some, the western coast of Hindustan; according to others, the shore of Ethiopia, Arabia Felix, and all the Indies.

——+——

ARTS AND INDUSTRY.—The Phœnicians, as in-
dustrious as enterprising, invented the art of
making glass, working the metals, carving ivory,
painting all sorts of vases, and making jewels.
(To them is also attributed the invention of writing and the alphabet, which they carried into
Greece and other colonies.) But the source of
their greatest wealth was the purple dye. Tradition says that a shepherd's dog, pressed by
hunger, having eaten some marine shell-fish, had
his mouth stained with a beautiful color. The
color having been extracted from other shell-fish
by the Phœnicians, they applied it to stuffs.
From that time purple became the insignia of
royalty among the Phœnicians.

RELIGION.—The principal divinity of the
Phœnicians was the same as that of the Assyrians
(—Baal, or the "sovereign master.)" He was
adored oftener under the name of *Baal-Moloch*,
or "sovereign destroyer," for they immolated in
his honor children of the noblest parentage,
either by casting them into a burning brazier or
shutting them up in a heated statue of the god.
The mothers deemed it a religious duty to look
on this spectacle with dry eyes and serene brow.
If they allowed a tear or sigh to escape them,
the sacrifice was less agreeable to the idol and
they could not obtain the desired effect, which
was to appease the anger of Baal and to unite the
victim with his divine being.

Sec. 2. CARTHAGE: *Her Conquests; War in Sicily in the Fourth and Fifth Centuries; Manners and Institutions of the Carthaginians.*

FOUNDATION OF CARTHAGE (872 B.C.); HER CONQUESTS.—Elissa, daughter of the king of Tyre, was called to the throne conjointly with her brother Pygmalion; but the latter refused to share the crown with her, and even assassinated her husband. The unfortunate princess decided to fly far from her country, and secretly embarked with her treasures and a number of Tyrians of the noblest families; hence her cognomen of *Dido*, or "fugitive." Arriving near Utica, the inhabitants would sell her only so much land as she could cover with the hide of a bull, but, having cut the hide into very narrow strips, she acquired a large portion of ground, on which was built Carthage, or the "new city."

Carthage, sometimes by arms, sometimes by money, extended little by little her territory at the expense of the neighboring nations. Her marts covered the African shore from the columns of Hercules, on the west, to Cyrenaica, on the east. The inhabitants of the latter country refused to contract their frontiers till after a disastrous war and the inhuman sacrifice of the Philæni, two brothers who permitted themselves to be buried alive to secure to their countrymen

—✠—

possession of the coveted frontier. The Carthaginians erected on the spot the altars of the Philæni.

After the destruction of Tyre by King Nabuchodonosor (574), Carthage occupied the following colonies : Malta; Sardinia, the Balearic Isles,
and a part of Spain. Thenceforward she became
a formidable power from the number of her vessels and soldiers, but chiefly from the merit of
her generals. Leagued with the Etruscans, she
delivered the isle of Corsica from the Phocians
of Marseilles. When Xerxes, King of Persia, invaded Greece, Carthage made an alliance with
him to drive the Greeks from Sicily.

WAR IN SICILY; BATTLE OF HIMERA (480).
—Hamilcar, landing in Sicily at the head of
three hundred thousand men, laid siege to Himera. The inhabitants called to their aid Gelon,
who possessed the authority in Syracuse. Gelon
set out immediately. He learned on the way
that Hamilcar expected on a certain day a body
of allied troops. Gelon, who was skilful and
cunning, chose from his army a body of men
equal in number to those expected by Hamilcar,
and sent them to that general as allies. These
soldiers, having been received into the camp of
the Carthaginians, threw themselves on Hamilcar, slew him, and set his ships on fire.

At the same time Gelon fell upon the Carthaginians, who, demoralized by the loss of their chief

and the burning of their fleet, were cut to pieces or made prisoners. This contest took place on the same day as the action at Thermopylæ. Carthage, humbled, sued for peace; she obtained it on condition of paying the costs of the war and of not sacrificing any more human victims to her divinities.

DESTRUCTION OF HIMERA (410) AND AGRIGENTUM (406).—The inhabitants of Segestes, menaced by those of Syracuse, called to their aid the Athenians, whose expedition into Sicily resulted disastrously, as we shall see in the history of Greece Then the Segestans, fearing the resentment of the other natives of Sicily, implored the aid of the Carthaginians. The latter eagerly seized an opportunity which would enable them to retrieve their former defeat. Hannibal, grandson of Hamilcar, who had been slain before Himera sixty years previously, besieged that city. It was taken, sacked, and destroyed to its very foundations. The conqueror, naturally cruel and revengeful, having forced three thousand prisoners to undergo every kind of ignominious punishment, murdered them all on the very spot where his grandfather had been killed by the soldiers of Gelon.

Their success rekindled in the Carthaginians the desire and hope of making themselves masters of the entire island. With their whole army they besieged Agrigentum, a rich and powerful

city. The siege lasted eight months. The besieged at length were forced by famine to
abandon their city, and even to leave behind the
old and sick. The Carthaginians, on entering
the city, secured an immense booty. A vast
number of pictures, vases, and statues of all
kinds were sent to Carthage, together with the
famous bull of Phalaris, the ancient tyrant of
Agrigentum.

DIONYSIUS THE ELDER (405-368); DEFEAT OF
HIMILCO BEFORE SYRACUSE (396).—Dionysius
the Elder, who was then tyrant of Syracuse, had
endeavored in vain to arrest the progress of the
Carthaginians. Necessity obliged him to conclude a disadvantageous peace ; but, aware of the
implacable hatred that the Sicilians felt toward
their ferocious conquerors, he profited by the
peace to make immense preparations. When he
believed himself able to undertake another war,
he gave the signal to massacre every Carthaginian
in Sicily. The Carthaginians, taken by surprise,
did not lose courage. Himilco, their general, the
same who had taken Agrigentum, landed in
Sicily at the head of a formidable army, recap-
tured all the cities that Dionysius had taken, and
forced the tyrant to shut himself up in Syracuse.

In the heat of his first successes the Carthaginian general thought he had nothing to fear.
He pillaged temples and destroyed the tombs
around the city, among others that of

-- ✤ --

He regarded Syracuse as his certain prey. But soon his pride and impiety met their due chastisement. The plague broke out in his army and made frightful ravages. Dionysius did not neglect this opportunity to attack his enemies. Already conquered by sickness, they made little resistance. Their fleet was nearly all burnt or taken. Night coming on, Himilco sent to Dionysius, requesting his permission to withdraw with the small remnants of his shattered army. But this permission could be obtained only for the Carthaginians, with whom Himilco stole away during the night, leaving the rest to the mercy of the conqueror. Arriving at Carthage, which was overwhelmed with grief, Himilco entered his house, shut the doors against the citizens, and even his wife and children, and, in despair, killed himself.

SUCCESS OBTAINED BY TIMOLEON OVER THE CARTHAGINIANS (345–343).—After the death of Dionysius the Elder there was great disorder in Syracuse. Dionysius the Younger, son of the tyrant, having been driven from the city, re-entered it with an armed force, and signalized his return by great cruelties. This seemed a favorable opportunity for the Carthaginians. They therefore sent thither Mago, their general, with a large fleet. In this extremity the Syracusans called to their aid the Corinthians. The latter sent them one of their citizens, Timoleon.

He arrived in Sicily with only a thousand soldiers; but the skill of the chief and the valor of
the soldiers compensated for numbers. The
Syracusans then found themselves in unwonted
stress—the Carthaginians master of their gates
and a part of the city, and Dionysius occupying
the citadel. Happily, the latter, being without
resources, restored the citadel, with its troops and
the provisions which remained. Upon this Mago
took alarm, and, weighing anchor, sailed for
Carthage, where he was tried and condemned.

A larger fleet was sent out and landed in Sicily.
Timoleon marched with only six thousand men
against seventy thousand Carthaginians, but, as
he knew that valor directed by prudence avails
more than numbers, he did not hesitate to give
battle. The Carthaginians were defeated, their
camp taken, and with it · immense treasures.
Timoleon, having concluded an honorable peace,
resigned his authority and retired to private life.
The Syracusans ever honored him as their father
and benefactor. At his death nothing was spared
to render his funeral magnificent, but the most
touching tribute were the tears and benedictions
shed in honor of his memory.

AGATHOCLES (317–289); HIS EXPEDITION INTO
AFRICA (311–307).—Agathocles was a Sicilian of
low birth. Supported by the Carthaginians, he
had seized the sovereignty of Syracuse shortly
after the death of Timoleon. When he saw Car-

thage becoming weakened, he declared himself against his benefactors. The latter, irritated, made a descent on Sicily and laid siege to Syracuse. The tyrant, abandoned by his allies because of his cruelty, and being greatly inferior in numbers to his enemy, conceived the daring project of carrying the war into Africa.

His profound secrecy on the subject is not less astonishing than the plan itself. He communicated it to no one, and at the moment of departure he alone knew whither the fleet was destined. When he had landed in Africa he represented to his troops that, to deliver their country, he had led them to Carthage, whose citizens were enervated by the indulgences of a voluptuous life, and that the riches of that proud city would become the reward of the conquerors. Seeing his soldiers disposed to follow him, he executed a second design more daring than the first—that of burning the fleet that had borne them to Africa, leaving his army no choice but to conquer or perish.

MOMENTARY SUCCESSES OF AGATHOCLES.— Agathocles lost no time, but advanced to Tunis, which he took by assault, and enriched his soldiers with the booty. Great was the alarm felt by the Carthaginians, who believed that the armies of the republic had been defeated before Syracuse. They hastily raised troops, but Agathocles cut them to pieces. The Syracusans

———✦———

hearing of this success, took courage, and fell upon the Carthaginians during the night, killed all that fell into their hands, and took their general, upon whom they inflicted the most cruel tortures. Agathocles, seeing his affairs in a prosperous state, thought of returning to Sicily. During his absence affairs in Africa had changed, and upon his return he found himself no longer able to command success. In this juncture, intent only on saving his own life, he basely deserted his army and returned to Syracuse. The soldiers of Agathocles avenged this treason by strangling his two sons and delivering them to the enemy. Shortly after the tyrant terminated by a miserable death a life that had been but a tissue of perfidy and cruelty (289).

Some years later the Carthaginians had to face in Sicily enemies more redoubtable—viz., Pyrrhus, King of Epirus, and afterwards the Romans. The *Punic wars* began in 264 B.C., and ended in 146 by the ruin of Carthage.

MANNERS OF THE CARTHAGINIANS.—In manners the Carthaginians were austere and stern even to cruelty, but their most marked traits were their ingenuity, cunning, and knavery. Their perfidy was so marked and so well known that it passed into a proverb, and became known as *fides Punica*, or Punic faith. These base qualities sprang from the thirst for riches, which was the soul of their enterprises. The education of Carthaginian youth consisted solely in writing, calculating, drawing up registers, and making out accounts.

MILITARY FORCES; MERCENARIES.—If Carthage was at first a commercial republic by situa tion and inclination, she soon became a warlike nation; first in order to sustain, and, lastly, to extend, her commerce. Her military force consisted principally of mercenary soldiers whom she bought in the neighboring states. With the aid of these she acquired provinces without depopulating her fields, impoverishing her marine, or interrupting her commerce. But these mercenaries did not possess true patriotism, and this polity has always been regarded as one of the principal causes of her ruin.

GOVERNMENT.—The government of Carthage, like that of Rome, consisted of three branches, which counterpoised and gave mutual assistance to each other: 1, two *suffetes*, or annual magistrates, who presided over public deliberations, judged important cases, and sometimes commanded the armies; 2, the *people*, who, less ambitious and less turbulent than those of Rome or Athens, left the care of public affairs to the senate, and took part in the deliberations only when that body was divided in opinion; 3, the *senate*, where affairs of consequence were debated and peace or war was declared. When the senators were divided in opinion, the case, as we have said, was brought before the people; but if their opinions were unanimous the senators decided definitively and without appeal. A striking proof of the wisdom of this law is given by the fact that for five hundred years there was in Carthage no considerable revolt, nor any tyrant who trampled upon the liberty of its people.

REVIEW QUESTIONS.

From whom were the Phœnicians descended? Where did they settle? Their chief city, and how was it called? By whom destroyed? What city inherited its power? What of Hiram? Of Jezabel? Why, when, and by whom was Tyre destroyed? Where did the Phœnicians establish colonies? How far did their commerce by land extend? What of their inventions? What can you say of their principal divinity? By whom was Carthage founded? By what stratagem was the site for that city obtained? What of the Philæni? What were the colonies of Carthage? With whom was it allied? Describe the battle of Himera. Its subsequent destruction. The siege of Agrigentum. By whom was Himilco afterwards defeated? What course did Dionysius pursue? What terms did he grant to the Carthaginians? Why was Mago sent to Syracuse? Who was Timoleon? His achievements in Syracuse? How honored in life and at his death? Who was Agathocles? How did he incur the enmity of Carthage? What daring plan did he conceive? Its momentary success? Its disastrous result? With whom were the Carthaginians afterwards at war? When did the *Punic Wars* commence? How and when did they end? What were the manners of the Carthaginians? Whence came the phrase *Punic* faith? The origin of their bad qualities? In what did the education of their youth consist? Why did Carthage become a warlike nation? In what did the strength of her military power consist? Did this afterwards become a source of weakness? What of the goverment of Carthage? Who were the suffetes and what were their duties? What powers were conferred on the senate? What remained to the people? How did this system operate?

CHAPTER V.

GREECE.

THE history of Greece, which was independent from the most remote times until the reign of Philip, King of Macedon, is divided into three periods : 1. The time anterior to the Median wars (2000–500 B.C.) 2. The Median wars (500–449 B.C.) 3. The Peloponnesian war, or the rivalry of Athens and Sparta, and the rivalry of Sparta and Thebes (449–360 B.C.)

Sec. 1. PRIMITIVE TIMES: *Sparta: Laws of Lycurgus ; Messenian Wars ; Athens ; Laws of Solon ; Pisistratus and his Sons (561–510 B.C.) ; Institutions and Customs of the Ancient Greeks.*

ORIGIN OF THE GREEKS ; THE PELASGI ; THE HELLENES, AND THE ORIENTAL COLONIES.—The Greeks, with a vanity common to many people, called themselves *Autochthones,* or "sprung from the soil where they dwelt." Holy Scripture, as well as science, teaches us that they came from the East, and were descendants of Javan, son of Japheth. (The first inhabitants of Greece were the Pelasgi, who had already occupied Asia Minor, and who soon spread to Italy (about 2000). It is believed that they founded the most ancient Greek cities—Sicyon and Mycenæ. To them

— -✠—

have been attributed the works ascribed to the Cyclops, because they seem to have belonged to a race of giants. These consist of enormous stones roughly hewn and placed one above the other without cement, and yet with so much art that they form indestructible monuments.

About the year 1600 B.C. the Hellenes also came to people Greece, whence the name Hellas. A tradition says that they are descended from Hellen, son of Deucalion. Hellen had three sons: Dorus, father of the Dorians; Æolus, father of the Æolians; and Xuthus, whose two sons, Ion and Achæus, were the progenitors of the Ionians and Achæans.

The Achæans, who at first acted the more brilliant part, ruled in the Peloponnesus, and numbered among their most illustrious chiefs Agamemnon and Menelaus. The Æolians appear to have occupied the centre and west of Greece. The rise and growth of the Ionians and Dorians, destined afterwards to become so famous under the name of Spartans and Athenians, is involved in obscurity.

From 1600 to 1300 B.C., according to ancient accounts, strangers from the East taught the Greeks useful arts and refined their rude manners. The Egyptian Cecrops, landing in Attica, divided the inhabitants into twelve small towns and gave them laws. The Phœnician Cadmus, having built the city named after him, and later the citadel of Thebes, taught the inhabitants the alphabet and writing.) The Egyptian Danaus, having settled in Argos, taught the art of tilling the soil, but he became more famous for the crime and punishment of his fifty daughters. The Phrygian Pelops extended his dominion over nearly all of southern Greece, called, from his name, Peloponnesus.

The Oriental origin of these personages has been doubted; but that the civilized Oriental nations exercised great influence over the sciences, arts, and customs of Greece is incontestable. For instance, the first four letters of the Greek alphabet exactly correspond to those of the Hebrews and Phœnicians.

HEROIC AGE: TROJAN WAR (1194–1184); HOMER.—The heroic age, from the fourteenth to the twelfth century, is signalized by the appearance of demi-gods and heroes who pertain less to history than to mythology. The history of their exploits is so marvellous that it is impossible to distinguish truth from error in the tissue of fables woven by the poetic imagination of the Greeks. All agree, however, in acknowledging four principal facts of this epoch:

1st, the *Argonautic Expedition*, undertaken in the thirteenth century to obtain from Colchis the "golden fleece," symbol of riches; 2d, the *War of the Seven Chiefs*, who, under the conduct of Adrastus, King of Argos, made vain efforts

to drive from Thebes King Eteocles, in favor
of his brother Polynices, both being sons of the
unfortunate Œdipus; 3d, the *War of the Epigoni,*
so called because the *children* of the chiefs slain
before Thebes, having leagued together ten years
later, seized that city, whence the national cause
triumphed over the descendants of the stranger
Cadmus; 4th and lastly, the famous *Trojan
War,* enkindled, according to the poets, by the
criminal passion of Paris, son of King Priam,
who carried off the beautiful Helen, wife of
Menelaus, King of Sparta.   The King of Mycenæ, Agamemnon, brother of Menelaus and grandson of Pelops, commanded the Greeks during a
siege of ten years, which ended in the destruction
of Troy.   This was the first triumph of warlike
Greece over Asia, enervated by luxury and voluptuousness (1184).*

The Trojan war, which armed all the Greeks
for a common interest, may be regarded as the
chief event of their history.   The genius of
Homer has cast over it an immortal splendor.
This great poet, who appears to have lived in the
tenth century, sang in his *Iliad* the story of
Achilles under the walls of Troy, and in his
Odyssey of the adventures of Ulysses returning

---

* Some historians place the siege of Troy in 1270, others in 1088.
In Greek history there is no certain date before the first Olympiad
(776), and the greater number of the dates are only approximative
before the Median wars.

to his island of Ithaca. We find in these two poems a vivid and striking picture of the customs of Greece at the close of the heroic times.)

INVASION OF THE DORIANS IN THE PELOPON-NESUS (1104) ; SELF-SACRIFICE OF CODRUS (1045).—{Twenty-four years after the destruction of Troy Aristodemus and two other descendants of Hercules, refugees in Doris, wished to return to the Peloponnesus, which had been wrested from their ancestors by the sons of Pelops. Placing themselves at the head of the Dorians, they constructed a fleet to traverse the gulf of Corinth, and landed unexpectedly on the Peloponnesian coast. (This was called "the return of the Heraclidæ" and "the invasion of the Dorians.") The greater part of the country fell under their power. The grandson of Agamemnon, Tisamenes, King of Sparta and Argos, withdrew with the Achæans to the country thenceforth called Achaia. The Æolians, driven from Messenia, emigrated to Asia Minor. Those Ionians who were stripped of their territory sought refuge among their brethren in Attica.*)

* The Æolians, having occupied the islands of Lesbos and Tenedos, spread into Mysia, and gave the name of Æolia to the country situated north of the Hermus. The Ionians, too straitened in Attica, seized upon that part of Asia Minor which lies between Caria and Lydia, and which thence was termed Ionia. At the same epoch the Dorians established themselves in the isles of Rhodes and Crete, and on the coast of Caria. From the eighth to the sixth century the Greeks founded other colonies in Sicily and southern Italy called

The Dorians, once established in their conquest, pursued the vanquished to Attica, where the Ionians advanced to meet them. The oracle at Delphi had promised victory to the nation which should lose its king. (The King of Athens, Codrus, the sixteenth successor of Cecrops, resolved to sacrifice himself for his people.) Disguised as a wood-cutter, he entered the enemy's camp and struck with his axe a soldier, who killed him on the spot. The Dorians, terrified at such devoted heroism, hastened to return to Peloponnesus. This was the first act of a long rivalry between the Spartans and the Athenians.

᷉KINGS OF SPARTA : LYCURGUS.—The Dorians, masters of Sparta, decided to establish a diarchy, or double dynasty; these dynasties were called the Agidæ and the Proclidæ.* (Lycurgus, fifth descendant of Procles, inherited the royal power at the death of his elder brother (898).) (The queen, his sister-in-law, offered, if he would espouse her, to secure him the crown by killing her offspring. Lycurgus rejected this criminal proposition, and Charilaüs, or "the joy of the people,"

Magna Græcia. Among other cities were the following : Messene, Syracuse, Agrigentum, Tarentum, Sybaris, Crotona, Cyrene, etc. ; in Africa, Cyrene ; in Chalcidia, Olynthus, Potidea, etc.

* Aristodemus, of the Heraclidæ, chief of the Dorians, perished in the invasion of the Peloponnesus. He left his twin sons, Eurysthenes and Procles (each equally dear to their mother), to reign conjointly. From Procles came the Proclidæ, called also Eurypontidæ, from his grandson, Eurypon ; the older branch, the Agidæ, received its name from Agis, son of Eurysthenes.

was soon after proclaimed king. The young prince grew up under the tutorship of his uncle, who governed the state with as much disinterestedness as skill. When Lycurgus was able to free himself from this duty he journeyed to the isle of Crete, and to Asia and Egypt, to consult the most distinguished men of those countries, which were then distinguished for the wisdom of their laws.

The Spartans recalled him to put an end to their discords. Lycurgus, with the support of the king, his nephew, gave them a new constitution. His work terminated, he declared to the people that he was going to set out on a journey, and requested them to promise on oath to be faithful to his laws till his return. Having obtained their solemn promise, he exiled himself voluntarily from his country, whither he never returned, and thus his countrymen were obliged to maintain for ever the laws he had given them.

POLITICAL LAWS; THE TWO KINGS; THE SENATE AND THE PEOPLE.—Lycurgus maintained the division of royalty between the two houses which claimed to descend from Hercules. The two kings were, in fact, but the first magistrates of the republic; they had the command of the armies, the principal functions in the religious ceremonies, and the presidency of the senate. The chief authority was vested in the senate, which was composed of twenty-eight

members, not less than sixty years of age, and named for life by the assembly of the people.)
This assembly met every month at the time of full moon, and had the right of adopting or rejecting the propositions of the kings and the senate. Five *Ephori,* or inspectors, were charged with the execution of the laws and to restrain the other powers.

The Spartans, who numbered about nine thousand, alone enjoyed all political rights. (The other inhabitants of Laconia were but their subjects, known as the Laconians, or slaves, called Helots, because the inhabitants of the city of Helos, in punishment of their revolt, had been reduced to the severest bondage.)

CIVIL LAWS; GOODS AND REPASTS IN COMMON. — Lycurgus wished to establish absolute equality among the Spartans. Their land was divided into as many portions as there were citizens.] Each portion, under the severest penalties, became inalienable property. To discourage the love of riches, this wise legislator prohibited the circulation of gold and silver and introduced iron coin, the value of which was fixed so low that a sum equivalent to one hundred dollars would have required a cart drawn by oxen to transport it.

[Lycurgus, wishing to banish luxury and intemperance, established public repasts, at which all the citizens partook of the frugal fare specified by law. The fare consisted ordinarily of a black broth little suited to tempt the appetite. The kings themselves were obliged to attend these repasts, and they were no better served than the humblest. One day, when Dionysius, the tyrant, exhibited repugnance for the dish set before him, "It lacks seasoning," was remarked. "What seasoning?" returned he. "Fatigue, hunger, and thirst season our meats." —

EDUCATION OF CHILDREN.—Lycurgus thought that children should belong more to the state than to their parents. He ordained that every new-born infant should be presented to the elders of the people. If he was deformed or incapable of becoming a soldier, he was at once condemned to death and thrown into a deep cavern near Mount Tagetus. If, on the contrary, he appeared vigorous, the elders returned him to his parents till the age of seven. The child then became the property of the state. His head was shaved, he went barefoot, and, in order to accustom him to military exercises, he was compelled to engage in bloody combats with his comrades. On the occasion of a certain festival in honor of Diana he was whipped till the blood ran down upon the altar, and often the sufferer expired under the lash.

(In this system of education letters, arts, commerce, and manufactures had no part; though the Spartan youth were orally instructed in a

knowledge of the laws, and modesty of deport-
ment was also inculcated, while conciseness of
speech was so carefully studied° as to give
rise to the term *laconic.* They were often
deprived of their customary food, in order that
they might have recourse to pilfering to appease
their hunger. If they were taken in the act,
they were punished, not for the theft, but for
their want of dexterity. Plutarch informs us
that one of them, having stolen a young fox, hid
it under his robe, and suffered it to gnaw out
his bowels rather than betray himself by any
sign of pain.)

CONDITION OF THE HELOTS; VICES OF THE
CONSTITUTION OF LYCURGUS.—The condition of
the slaves was nowhere so miserable as in the
city of Sparta. Covered with the skins of wild
beasts, which served to distinguish them, they
were employed in the most painful works with
no other reward than contempt and the most
cruel treatment. Every year these unhappy beings received in public a certain number of
strokes, that they might the more keenly realize
their hard lot. When their term of service was
ended they could not be admitted into the rank
of citizens, as the law prohibited this. On one
occasion two thousand of them were declared
free because they had shown remarkable valor in
a combat; the following night they were massacred.

On certain occasions the young Spartans were invited to hunt the Helots, and their skill was reckoned by the number of their victims. Interest, in default of humanity, would have put a stop to this sanguinary play, if they had lacked slaves; but these numbered 220,000 in the city of Sparta alone.

Historians have greatly praised the military courage of the Spartans, their love of country, and their respect for the aged; but these qualities cannot counterbalance what was vicious in their manners and legislation, such as their cruelty towards their slaves, the judicial murder of infants, their barbarous education, communism legally established, theft dignified as a virtue, and the most revolting contempt of the marriage and family ties. Thus the constitution of Lycurgus, which sacrificed everything for the benefit of the state, should be regarded as one of the worst ever framed.

FIRST MESSENIAN WAR (744–724); ARISTODEMUS.—The Spartans, educated to love nothing but their country, rendered themselves notorious in antiquity by their hatred of all stranger nations, especially the neighboring states. Having no respect for the rights of others, they refused to listen to a rich Messenian who complained of the murder of his son and the rapine of his flocks. The Messenian endeavored to retaliate, and the Spartans took advantage of this to invade Messenia, a fertile country which they wished to add to Laconia.) After two battles the Messenians, weakened by famine and plague, retired to Mount Ithomus, at the northwest of Messene, their capital.

An oracle had announced that to deliver themselves from their disasters they must immolate a virgin of royal blood; but she upon whom the lot fell having fled to Sparta, under the conduct of her father, Aristodemus, in a transport of madness, immolated his own daughter. Proclaimed king by his countrymen, he defeated the Spartans and sacrificed to Jupiter three hundred prisoners, with their king, Theopompus. A new oracle decreed yet another victim. Aristodemus, discouraged by some reverses and tortured by just remorse, stabbed himself over the tomb of his daughter. The Messenians, after a war of twenty years, capitulated, and consented to give every year the half of their harvests, and to repair in mourning garments to Sparta to attend at the obsequies of their kings and principal magistrates.

SECOND WAR (684–668); ARISTOMENES.—The Messenians, exasperated by a servitude which had lasted for forty years, chose for king the brave Aristomenes, who destroyed the army of the Lacedæmonians. The conqueror, entering Sparta alone in the middle of the night, suspended in the temple of Minerva a shield with the following inscription: "Aristomenes consecrates to Minerva these spoils of the Lacedæmonians."

Sparta, terrified, consulted the oracle at Delphi, which responded that she would be saved by a chief from Athens. Athens, little concerned for the safety of Sparta, sent her a lame schoolmaster, who was a poet and passed for a simpleton. The Spartans, vanquished in three encounters, were about to abandon the struggle, when Tyrteus, the Athenian schoolmaster, reanimated their courage by his warlike songs. The Messenians, beaten in their turn, and betrayed by the king of Arcadia, sought refuge in the city of Ira, at the north of Messene.

Aristomenes continued to make daring assaults on the enemy. It is related that one day, having fallen into their hands, he was thrown into a pit in which they cast malefactors. By a miracle alone he survived the fall. Aristomenes well-nigh despaired of escaping, when suddenly he heard a slight noise, and perceived, in the gloom, a fox devouring corpses. Rightly judging that the animal could not have come thither without some way of ingress, he seized it, and, creeping after it, came to an opening above ground. Soon new exploits betokened his presence among the Messenians. The famous siege had lasted eleven years, when the besiegers, favored by a storm, carried by assault the defences of Ira. Aristomenes, having eluded them, vainly essayed

to surprise the city of Sparta, and withdrew to
the island of Rhodes. As to the Messenians,
some went to found a colony in Sicily, but a
greater number were taken and reduced to servitude.   Their descendants united with the Helots
against Sparta, of whom twenty thousand perished in an earthquake ; but this third Messenian
war (464–454) terminated, as did the two others,
in the triumph of Sparta.

ATHENS : THE ARCHONS ; DRACO (624) AND
SOLON (593).—After the death of King Codrus
(1045) the Athenians abolished royalty, under
pretext that no one was worthy of being his successor.   Instead of a king they appointed an
archon, or governor, for life, whose authority
was in the end limited to ten years, and finally to
one (684), when it was shared by nine archons.
Such restricted power was not sufficient to curb
turbulent and factious spirits.   The troubles
which ensued taught the Athenians that true
liberty consists in a dependence on justice and
reason.   They therefore sought a legislator in
Draco, a man of acknowledged wisdom and integrity (622). He published some laws whose rigor
was so extreme as to punish the smallest offence,
as well as the most enormous crime, with death.
This code suffered the same fate as all violent
measures: it did not last, and the Athenians
were obliged to have recourse to Solon.   The
rich agreed to the change because Solon was rich.

and the poor because he was good. He was, in fact, the most moderate and virtuous man of his age. His merits placed him among the seven sages of Greece, who rendered their age so illustrious. *

LAWS OF SOLON.—Solon, being named archon, abolished the laws of Draco. Having declared that the goods of the debtor and not his person should be given in pay, he released all the poor who had been sold as slaves to their creditors. (By other laws, wiser than those of Lycurgus, he protected property, prohibited theft under severe penalties, secured family rights, prescribed the labors and softened the rigorous lot of the slaves, but without according to them all the rights that humanity claims.) There were then two hundred thousand slaves in Athens alone.

Solon divided all the citizens into four classes, the three first having the exclusive possession of offices and magistracies; but to counterbalance this exclusion of the poor (the fourth class) from executive government he gave them the right of voting in public assemblies. This privilege might at first sight appear of little consequence,

* The seven sages of Greece were Solon, Thales of Miletus, Pittacus of Mitylene, Bias, Cleobulus, Chilo, and the laborer Myson, or, according to some historians, Periander of Corinth. These sages communicated to each other their thoughts on the principal truths of morality and policy. To them are attributed many wise maxims, such as " Know thyself," etc. We must not forget that Solon and the other sages of Greece, considered virtuous among the pagans, were not exempt from vices condemned by Christianity.

yet, on account of their numbers, it was most important, since the greatest affairs of state were to be decided in the assemblies of the people. But, in order to preserve a sort of equilibrium, Solon established a senate, and provided that a subject should previously receive the sanction of the senate before being discussed in the general assemblies. It was in allusion to this that Anacharsis, a Scythian, said one day to Solon: "I wonder you should empower wise men only to deliberate, and leave the decision to fools."

THE AREOPAGUS.—The Areopagus, a tribunal established from time immemorial, at first judged only criminal cases. Solon enlarged its powers; no one was admitted save men of superior integrity, wisdom, and experience, and thus it soon became the most celebrated tribunal in the world. Criminal cases were tried only at night, that the judges might not be moved by the sight of the accuser or the accused. Entrance to the tribunal was for a long time refused to lawyers, and they were finally permitted to enter only on condition that they would banish from their discourses all perorations, exordiums, or other rhetorical effects. When the members of the Areopagus had finished the trial of a cause, their votes were placed some in the *urn of death,* others in the *urn of mercy.* Their judgments were received with great reverence.

—+—

USURPATION . OF PISISTRATUS (561–527).— Solon, having made his countrymen swear they would observe his laws for ten years, quit his country and went to visit Asia Minor, the isle of Cyprus, and Egypt. On his return he found Athens again a prey to civil feuds and factions. Soon after he had the grief to see its liberties subverted by his relative Pisistratus, himself an Athenian, who, under the veil of moderation and beneficence, cherished an unbounded ambition. One day wounding himself, he caused his body, covered with blood, to be transported to the market-place, and roused the beholders to indignation by giving them to understand that he had been thus treated by his enemies on account of his zeal for the republic. The people, believing him, appointed forty guards to protect his person. Pisistratus augmented the number, and thus made himself absolute master of Athens (561).

The power he thus acquired he exercised with mildness, and signalized his administration by cultivating a taste for letters and arts. As he was unjustly accused of murder, instead of proceeding cruelly against his calumniators, he went in person to justify himself before the Areopagus. The Greeks did not yet know the entire poems of Homer, portions only of which were recited by the *rhapsodes*, or wandering minstrels. Pisistratus is said to have made the first complete collection of the fragments of the *Iliad* and *Odyssey.*)

THE SONS OF PISISTRATUS; ABOLITION OF ROYALTY (510) AND ESTABLISHMENT OF THE ARCHONSHIP.—The two sons of Pisistratus, Hippias and Hipparchus, inherited his power, and for thirteen years (527–514) exercised it with mildness. But two Athenian youths allied by the closest friendship, Harmodius and Aristogiton, wishing to avenge a personal injury done the former, assassinated Hipparchus at a grand feast celebrated in honor of Minerva.) Harmodius was slain on the spot by the guards of Hipparchus, Aristogiton also being shortly afterwards seized and put to death. These unworthy persons were afterwards honored by the Athenians as victims in the cause of liberty. Hippias, growing suspicious and cruel, was driven from the city, and royalty was abolished in the year which preceded the fall of the Tarquins at Rome.

The Athenians re-established popular government. The archon Clisthenes, of the illustrious family of Alcmæonidæ, increased the number of tribes from four to ten, and that of the senators from four hundred to five hundred. The senators, when in the exercise of their functions, were supported at the public expense in the *Prytaneum,* a public edifice which served also as a retreat for those who deserved well of their

—+—

country. To Clisthenes is also attributed the institution of (ostracism, a solemn vote so called because of a shell coated with wax on which the citizens wrote the name of the accused if they condemned him to exile.) The Spartans disliked and opposed these reforms.

Besides Messene Sparta had conquered a part of Arcadia and Argos ; in fact, she possessed two-thirds of the Peloponnesus. Athens was. her most powerful rival, the former extending her dominion over the isle of Eubæa and in the Cyclades. Adjoining Persia, she determined to intervene between that country and Asia Minor, thus furnishing a pretext for the Median wars.

RELIGION AND FESTIVALS OF THE GREEKS.— It is observable that in all ages and in all nations, however opposite in character, inclinations, and manners, a belief in a Supreme Being has always existed, and this belief has always been evinced by external forms and ceremonies. So universal a sentiment could be implanted in the human heart· only by the Author of all being. But the vices and frailties of the human heart have strangely perverted this ennobling sentiment. The Greeks,· especially, had for religion a monstrous collection. of infamous absurdities. They erected altars to. the adulterous Jupiter, the robber Mercury, the. impure Venus, and a thousand other divinities, the patrons of vice. An infinite number of festivals were celebrated in their honor.

The worship of Bacchus, the god of wine, was especially celebrated at Athens. At these cere-monies nothing was seen but dancing, drunken-ness, and debauchery. Among the most famous in pagan antiquity was the festival of Ceres, at Eleusis. It was of nine days' duration and was celebrated every fifth year. It was a capital offence to reveal its secrets to those who were not initiated. This austere law of silence was made to conceal the disorders and abominations which accompanied the celebration of pagan mysteries.

ORACLE OF DELPHI.—No country was ever more productive of oracles than Greece, and the most celebrated was that of Apollo at Delphi. This god had a priestess who answered those who came to consult him, but she could not pro-phesy till she was frenzied by the exhalations from the sanctuary of Apollo. The god was not always in an inspiring mood. At first he in-spired her but once a year; but later on he was prevailed upon to do so every month. As soon as the divine vapor began to be diffused the hair of the priestess stood upright, her eyes sparkled, and froth issued from her lips. She uttered almost inarticulate words, which the assistants carefully collected and arranged in order.

The characteristic feature of these oracles was equivocation and obscurity, so that the same an-swer might be equally applied to different events.

—✛—

Thus, when Crœsus was on the point of attacking the Medes, he consulted the oracle at Delphi upon the success of the war. He was answered that he would ruin a great empire. What empire—his own or that of his enemy? He was to guess that, but whatever the event might be, the oracle could not fail of being in the right. The same may be said of the god's answer to Pyrrhus ·

" Aio te, Æacides, Romanos vincere posse ";

that is, Pyrrhus might conquer the Romans, or the Romans might conquer Pyrrhus; and he naturally gave to the oracle the construction that flattered his ambition, but was vanquished.

AMPHICTYONIC COUNCIL.—The Amphictyonic Council, the origin of which has been attributed to Amphictyon, king of Thessaly, was an association, political as well as religious, formed by twelve cities of Greece, to judge all important cases, and especially attempts against the rights of men or the sanctuary at Delphi. Each city had two votes in the council, which met twice a year, in the spring at Delphi and in the autumn at Thermopylæ. All affairs were decided by a plurality of votes.

Sometimes the Amphictyones decreed a national recompense to such as had deserved it. Thus, the council ordered a magnificent monument to be erected to Leonidas and his three hundred Spartans, with this inscription, composed by the poet Simonides :

"Go, stranger, and to listening Sparta tell
That here obedient to her laws we fell."

But they more frequently exercised their authority against those whose traitorous or impious conduct exposed them to the penalty of the law. Such was the chastisement inflicted on the Phocians for having ploughed up a part of the land consecrated to Apollo. Philip of Macedon was charged to execute this sentence of the Amphictyones, and received in reward the two suffrages of the Phocians in the Amphictyonic Council.

GAMES AND COMBATS; ATHLETES.—Games and combats formed a part of the religion of the ancients. The Greeks, naturally warlike, introduced these exercises in order to render their youth robust and intrepid in close fight. There were four games celebrated in Greece : the Isthmian, near Corinth, in honor of Neptune ; the Nemean, in Argos, in honor of Hercules ; the Pythian, at Delphi, in honor of Apollo, conqueror of the serpent Python; and the Olympian, at Olympia, the most famous and celebrated every four years. In 776 a foot-racer named Corœbus carried off the prize ; the date is noteworthy, as from that year the Greeks reckon their Olympiads, or periods of every four years.

Those who were permitted to contend in the

games were called athletes, and were required to
be of Hellenic blood, freemen, and of irreproach-
able character. The games consisted of horse
and foot races; leaping; throwing the discus, or
quoit; wrestling and boxing, and combinations
of these. Their diet was very austere: they
lived upon dry figs, walnuts, soft cheese, and
coarse bread, and were interdicted the use of
wine. In wrestling the combatants were rubbed
with oil, matched two against two, and each endeavored to throw his adversary on the ground.
In boxing the combatants armed their hands
with the cestus, a kind of glove made, according
to Virgil, of leather and lead, which added
weight to their blows. The *pancratium* united
boxing and wrestling, and was the rudest and
most dangerous of the combats; in fact, these
exercises frequently ended in the maiming, and
sometimes even in the death, of the combatants.
The discus was a kind of quoit, of wood, stone,
lead, or any other metal, and extremely heavy.
He that threw the discus farthest was the victor.
There were three kinds of races: the chariot,
the horse, and the foot race. Races held the
foremost rank among the ancients, kings themselves contending for the prize.

The conqueror was crowned before all Greece
and was conducted with great pomp to his own
country. He made his entry not through the
gates, but through a breach purposely made in

the walls of his native city. The rest of his life he was maintained at the expense of the country. Poets sang his praise, and statues were erected in his honor. To be crowned victor at the Olympian games was the highest honor attainable by a Greek. Indeed, there are instances on record in which altars were erected and sacrifices offered to conquerors at these games.

Sec. 2. MEDIAN WARS (500–449 B.C.): *First War—Battle of Marathon* (490 B.C.); *Second War—Battles of Salamis* (480 B.C.), *Platæa, and Mycale* (479 B.C.); *Third War—Victories of Cimon; Treaty of Peace* (449 B.C).

ORIGIN OF THE MEDIAN WARS.—Darius I., king of Persia, having extended his conquests to Macedonia, threatened the independence of Greece. He soon found a pretext for attacking her in the revolt of the Ionians. The province of the latter was one of the richest in Asia Minor, and had borne with impatience the yoke which Cyrus had imposed. At the instigation of Aristagoras, tyrant of Miletus, the Ionians hastened to throw it off. As they were originally from Attica, they easily obtained aid from the Athenians. The latter, moreover, were incensed against the king of Persia for giving refuge to Hippias, son of Pisistratus. Their troops, united to those of Ionia, surprised the city of Sardis and burnt

———✠———

·it (500). Darius on hearing this seized his bow and, shooting an arrow towards heaven, cried: "Great Jupiter, may I one day revenge myself on the Athenians." Fearing that he might forget his projects of vengeance, he charged an officer to call out to him in a loud voice, whenever he was at table, "Sire, remember the Athenians."

This was the origin of that famous war of fifty years, in which Darius and his two successors endeavored to crush a people jealous of their liberty. It is one of the grandest spectacles that ancient history offers us. We see two weak cities, Athens and Sparta, abandoned by their allies and with no other support than their courage, resisting nearly the whole of Asia, destroying numerous fleets, putting to flight immense armies, and remaining victorious over the most formidable power that the world had yet seen.

FIRST WAR: BATTLE OF MARATHON (490).—Darius, having quelled the revolt in Ionia, charged Mardonius, his son-in-law, with the conduct of large forces, both by land and sea, against the Greeks; but the Brygi attacked and killed many of the army, and a furious tempest dispersed the fleet while doubling Mount Athos (492).

The Persian king, far from being discouraged, embarked a more powerful army than before.

He was preceded by heralds, who demanded in all the principal cities land and water, in the name of the Persian king. It was in this manner the Persians were accustomed to exact submission from those whom they conquered. Many cities were intimidated and yielded to the demand. But at Athens and Sparta the heralds were badly treated; they were thrown into a deep ditch, and bade to take the land and water they desired.

This new insult roused to the highest pitch the resentment of the Persians. Setting sail from the shores of Asia with six hundred vessels they directed their course to Attica, and landed one hundred and ten thousand men, under Datis and Artaphernes, near Marathon, a small town ten miles from Athens. The Athenians could muster only ten thousand soldiers, but their courage rendered them a host. Aristides, whose rare virtues gave him the surname of Just, was at the head of the army with Miltiades and eight other chiefs. When his turn had come to take the command he resigned it to Miltiades, as the more skilful general; his colleagues did the same, and this generous conduct helped Miltiades to form his plan for the approaching conflict with equal energy and prudence.

He arranged his army in a straight line, covering its flanks with the trunks of trees. The

Athenians, thus posted, did not await the onset of the enemy; as soon as the signal was given, they rushed with fury on the Persian troops. The battle was fierce and obstinate, as the Persians outnumbered the Athenians ten to one; but the two wings of the latter, having defeated those of the Persians, attacked the front and soon put the enemy to rout. The Persians betook themselves to flight, not towards their camp but to their ships, that they might escape the sword of the conquerors. Meanwhile an Athenian soldier, reeking with the blood of the enemy, quitted the army and ran to Athens, to carry to his fellow-citizens the happy news of the victory. He uttered but these words, "Rejoice! the victory is ours," and fell dead.

INGRATITUDE OF THE ATHENIANS.—The gratitude felt by the Athenians towards Miltiades was of short duration. Soon after the battle of Marathon he was accused of treason and condemned to pay a fine of fifty talents (nearly fifty-three thousand dollars), and, being unable to pay so considerable a sum, was thrown into prison, where he perished miserably from a wound he had received in battle. Aristides experienced in his turn the fickleness of his countrymen. By the intrigues of Themistocles he was ostracized and condemned to an exile of ten years.

XERXES (485–472); EXPEDITION AGAINST THE GREEKS.—Darius, dying, left the war to be carried on by his son Xerxes. Xerxes had a brother who disputed with him the crown. They agreed to refer their difference to their uncle, and the latter gave judgment in favor of Xerxes. While the dispute lasted, the two brothers exhibited a truly fraternal friendship, and when Xerxes was proclaimed king, his brother was the first to prostrate himself before him and acknowledge him as his master (485).

Xerxes did not long preserve that wonderful moderation which rendered him so worthy of the crown. No sooner was he seated on the throne than he turned his arms against the Greeks. He resolved to cut a pass through Mount Athos, which impeded the march of his army. He wrote the following foolish letter to the mountain: "Proud and aspiring Athos, do not dare to put rocks and stones that cannot be cut in the way of my workmen, else I will cut thee entirely down and throw thee into the sea." Xerxes had caused a bridge of boats to be built upon the Hellespont for the passage of his forces from Asia into Europe; but a violent storm arose and broke the bridge to piece. The king, transported with fury, ordered men to lash the sea with one hundred s[?] a whip, and had all who had been [?] the undertaking put to death. H other bridges to be built, on which the whole Persian army, amounting to two millions of men, passed.

LEONIDAS AT THERMOPYLÆ (480).—Most of the Greeks immediately submitted to the Persian monarch; Sparta, Athens, and Platæa alone dared to resist.

The danger seemed but to reanimate their courage. Their fleet consisted of but three hundred vessels, and Leonidas, with only four thousand men, occupied the defile of Thermopylæ, a narrow pass of Mount Œta, which was the only way by which the Persians could enter Greece. When Xerxes approached the pass he was surprised to find its passage disputed. He endeavored to gain over Leonidas by magnificent promises, but failing, tried menaces, and wrote him a letter ordering him to deliver his arms. Leonidas, in a style and spirit truly laconic, answered, " Come and take them."

During three days Xerxes tried to carry the pass by assault; failing to do so, he was filled with despondency, when an inhabitant of the country came to him and revealed a secret path leading to an eminence which overlooked the Spartan forces. Xerxes quickly despatched a detachment thither. Leonidas, seeing it now impossible to withstand the enemy, dismissed his allies; but himself and his three hundred Lacedæmonians resolved to die at their post. The Spartans, overwhelmed by numbers, heroically perished, except one man, who escaped to Sparta, where he was regarded as a traitor, and despised and shunned by everybody.

BATTLE OF SALAMIS (480).—Xerxes, after burning and ravaging the cities of Phocia, hastened to Athens, which he found deserted and reduced to ashes. The Persian fleet likewise was preparing to combat the Greeks. At the same time there arose a division among the Grecian commanders concerning the place for engaging the enemy. Some of them, among whom was Eurybiades, were for advancing near the isthmus of Corinth; others alleged that it would be betraying their country to abandon so advantageous a post as Salamis. As Themistocles supported with warmth this last opinion, Eurybiades lifted his staff in a menacing manner, "Strike," said the Athenian, "but hear me." His moderation, joined to his force of reasoning, gave weight to the advice which saved Greece.

Both sides prepared for a naval engagement. Xerxes caused a throne to be erected on a height commanding a view of the sea. The Persians, knowing that their king was watching their movements, attacked the Greeks with much impetuosity. But the manner in which they were received soon cooled their ardor, and they quickly took to flight, although infinitely superior in numbers to their pursuers.

Artemesia, queen of Caria and allied to Xerxes, alone displayed resolution and courage. After extraordinary efforts, seeing herself pursued by an Athenian ship, she hung out Grecian colors and attacked a Persian ship, commanded by a prince with whom she had a quarrel, and sunk it. This led her pursuers to believe that her vessel belonged to the Grecian fleet, and they ceased the pursuit. The Persians lost a great number of vessels, either taken or sunk. Xerxes fled to the Hellespont; but he found the bridge broken, and he whose armies and fleets covered land and sea a little while before, now stole away to Asia, almost alone, in a little fishing boat.

BATTLES OF PLATÆA AND MYCALE (479).—Mardonius, the brother-in-law of Xerxes, remained in Greece with a body of three hundred thousand men. He endeavored to detach the Athenians from the other Greeks, but Aristides, then first archon, made the following haughty reply: "Know," said he, pointing to the sun, "that as long as that luminary shall continue his course the Athenians will be mortal enemies to the Persians, and will not cease to take vengeance on them for ravaging their lands and burning their houses and temples." The war continued with an ardor which excited still more among the Greeks the thirst of vengeance. The Athenians and Lacedæmonians, commanded respectively by Aristides and Pausanias, met the Persian army near Platæa, in Bœotia. The battle was very fierce and the victory long in doubt, but the Persian general perishing in the conflict, his troops lost courage and fled. The Greeks had made such carnage that of the three hundred thousand men who composed the Persian army not fifty thousand escaped.

On the same day on which the Greeks fought the battle of Platæa their naval forces obtained a memorable victory in Asia over the remainder of the Persian fleet. The vanquished retired to the promontory of Mycale, where an army of one hundred thousand men was stationed; the Greeks pursued them, forced their camp, and burnt all their vessels. Xerxes, hearing the news of these two great disasters, quitted Sardis with great haste and retired to Susa. From this period, so glorious for the Greeks, no Persian army dared to cross the Hellespont (479).

THEMISTOCLES REBUILDS ATHENS.—The Athenians, being delivered from the Persians, thought of rebuilding their city and surrounding it with strong walls. The Lacedæmonians, secretly jealous of a power that already rivalled theirs, represented that the common interests of Greece required that there should be no fortified city out of the Peloponnesus, lest it should afterwards become an arsenal for barbarians. But Themistocles, who penetrated their design, was in his turn not less cunning. He proposed to the Athe-

nians to send a deputation to Sparta to settle
the affair. He caused himself to be named one
of the deputies, and warned the senate not to
let his colleagues set out with him, but to send
them one after the other. Meanwhile they
urged on the work at Athens day and night.
To gain more time, Themistocles, on arriving at
Sparta, did not press for an audience; he waited,
he said, for his colleagues. The Spartans made
great complaints to Themistocles of the work
carried on at Athens; he denied the fact, and
bade them send other deputies, to inform themselves better on the subject. At the same time
he secretly instructed the Athenians to retain
the Spartan envoys as hostages till he and his
colleagues returned. At last he declared to the
senate that the Athenians had thought it necessary for their security to fortify their city with
walls. The Lacedæmonians were exceedingly
displeased with this declaration, but, distrusting
their strength, dissembled their anger (478).
Themistocles returned to Athens, where he built
and fortified the Piræus.

DEATH OF ARISTIDES AND EXILE OF THEMIS-
TOCLES; ARTAXERXES LONGIMANUS (472–424).—
Themistocles was full of ardor for the aggran-
dizement of his country, and scrupled not at
the means. One day he declared in a public
assembly that he had conceived an important
project, but would not make it known to the

people.　Aristides was appointed to confer with him.　Themistocles disclosed a plan for burning the allied (or, according to another authority, the Lacedæmonian) fleet, thus making Athens absolute mistress of the sea.　Aristides, after hearing Themistocles, returned to the assembly and declared that nothing could be more advantageous, but nothing more dishonorable and unjust, than the design of his colleague.　The people thereupon unanimously rejected the proposal of Themistocles, without even enquiring in what it consisted.　Aristides died some time after, mourned by the Athenians as the best man of their city.　As for Themistocles, his passionate thirst for glory rendered him odious to his countrymen, and he was banished from Athens by the ostracism (473).

While Greece was repairing the evils caused by the Persian invasion Xerxes, rendering himself despicable by his luxury and effeminacy, was assassinated, and was succeeded by his son, Artaxerxes Longimanus * (473).　History boasts much of his goodness and generosity.　Themistocles took refuge at the court of this prince, who

* Artaxerxes I. published in 454 the celebrated edict which permitted the Jews to rebuild the walls of Jerusalem ; and here begin the seventy weeks of years predicted by the prophet Daniel which determined the epoch of the advent of the Messias.　Artaxerxes was long regarded as the Assuerus of the Bible who repudiated Queen Vasthi to espouse Esther, but later researches prove that Assuerus was none other than Xerxes I., who espoused Esther after his expedition into Greece.

treated him with marked kindness, three flourishing towns being assigned for his maintenance.

The Athenians, ever at war with the Persians, endeavored to repair the loss of Themistocles by bestowing on Cimon the command of their armies (471).

VICTORIES OF CIMON; TREATY OF PEACE (441).—Cimon was the son of Miltiades. From the time that he began to take part in public affairs he was filled with every impulse that was good and noble. He was not inferior either to his father or Themistocles in military science, and he excelled both in modesty, disinterestedness, love of justice, and zeal for his country. The Persian power suffered more from Cimon than from any other commander. After having driven the enemy from the Grecian isles, he pursued them to their own country. At the mouth of the Eurymedon he attacked and defeated their fleet, although more numerous than his own. On the same day he landed his army, attacked the Persian forces and cut them to pieces (470).

Cimon pushed on his conquests with such vigor that Artaxerxes, finding no general to oppose him, proposed to Themistocles to take the field against the Athenians. Not wishing to appear ungrateful to a king who had loaded him with favors, nor to take the traitor's part against

—*—

his country, it is said he poisoned himself by
drinking bull's blood (466).   The king still endeavored to oppose Cimon, but suffered so many
disasters that he was obliged to conclude a treaty
of peace, the terms of which were as humiliating
to the Persians as glorious for the Greeks.   The
former lost all the Greek cities of Asia Minor,
and promised to withdraw their fleets and armies
far from the coast of Greece.

Sec. 3. PELOPONNESIAN WAR (431-404 B.C.);
*Preponderance of Athens; Pericles; Alci-
biades; Athens taken* (404 B.C.); *Retreat of
the Ten Thousand* (401-400 B.C.); *Socrates;
Preponderance of Sparta; Rivalry between
Athens and Sparta.*

CAUSE OF THE WAR; PERICLES; PREPONDER-
ANCE OF ATHENS.—The Greeks, who had united the better to defend themselves from the formidable Persian host, now that they were victorious, hastened to break their treaty of alliance
and turn against each other the arms with which
they had so successfully combated the barbarians.
The power and superiority of Athens caused much
jealousy on the part of Sparta and many other cities, and led to the Peloponnesian war.

Athens had attained her preponderance since
the Greeks, despite the opposition of Sparta, had
chosen Aristides and Cimon to direct public

---

affairs.* Thenceforth they pledged themselves to pay annually to the Athenians a considerable sum to defray the expenses of the war and to build ships. Cimon had availed himself of this to conquer the Persians. Pericles, who succeeded him in the direction of affairs, employed the money of the allies only to enhance the grandeur of Athens.

The military courage of Pericles equalled that of his father Xanthippus, one of the victors of Mycale; but his sweet, insinuating manner was most admired. He possessed eloquence in an eminent degree, a talent which he regarded as next in importance to virtue in one who aspired to guide and govern a republican people. The epoch of his government was the most splendid in the history of Athens.

Pericles caused the Parthenon, the temple of Minerva, the *propylæa*, or vestibule, to the Acropolis, or citadel, and the Odeon, or music-hall, to be constructed. All the great works of this epoch were placed under the direction of Phidias,

---

* This choice took place after the death of the Spartan Pausanias, who took a principal part in the battle of Platæa. Inflated with success, he secretly treated with Xerxes to obtain the title of king at the price of the enthralment of Greece. Convicted of treason and condemned to death, he took refuge in the temple of Minerva. The entrance was immediately blocked up with large stones, the first of which was brought by the criminal's mother. The roof of the temple was taken off and Pausanias left to die of hunger. Sparta was thus deprived of the only man who could successfully oppose Aristides and Cimon.

the most celebrated sculptor of antiquity. His statues of Minerva and of Jupiter Olympus were especially admired. Letters as well as the arts flourished in the age of Pericles. About this time Athens possessed the famous dramatic poets Æschylus, Sophocles, Euripides, and Aristophanes; the masterly historians Herodotus, Thucydides, and Xenophon; the eloquent orators Isocrates and Lysias; the eminent sculptors and painters Phidias, Callicrates, Apollodorus, Zeuxis, and Parrhasius; the great philosophers Anaxagoras, Socrates, and Plato; Hippocrates, the ablest physician of antiquity; and Pericles himself, in whom were blended the characteristics of the admiral, the general, the statesman, and the orator.

COMMENCEMENT OF THE WAR (431); THE TWO INVASIONS.—But this magnificence excited the jealousy of the allies of the Athenians. They complained that the contributions paid for the common safety of Greece were employed in superfluous embellishments, and that Athens was thus become the richest city. Pericles and the Athenians answered that as long as they protected their allies they were not obliged to render to them an account of the use made of the contributions. This haughty response satisfied no one, and Athens, fearing a revolt, ordered Potidæa, one of the hostile cities, to level her walls and give hostages. Potidæa refused to

—✛—

obey an order she considered tyrannical, and this was the signal for revolt (431).

The Lacedæmonians, always jealous of the prosperity of Athens, hastened to declare against her; also the Thebans, the Corinthians, and nearly all of Peloponnesus. Archidamus, king of Sparta, entered Attica followed by an army of sixty thousand men. The Athenians, by the advice of Pericles, shunned all engagement with an enemy far superior in numbers, and allowed them to advance to the very gates of the city. Meanwhile, the Athenian fleet, commanded by Pericles, sailed toward Peloponnesus, and, ravaging all the coast, compelled the Lacedæmonians and their allies to return and defend their own country.

PLAGUE AT ATHENS; DEATH OF PERICLES (428).—In the beginning of the second campaign the Lacedæmonians returned to Attica and laid it waste. But the plague made still greater devastation in Athens. The most robust constitutions were unable to withstand its attacks; the houses and very temples were filled with the dead; everywhere were visible the frightful ravages of the pestilence. Pericles himself was attacked and soon reduced to the last extremity. As he lay at the point of death, and apparently unconscious, his friends, conversing around his bed, began to extol his exploits. Suddenly Pericles broke silence. "You forget," said he,

—✛—

"the most honorable circumstance of my life—
that I have never caused any citizen to put on
mourning." It is easy to conceive how much
this great man was regretted. The faults which
the Athenians committed after his death, even
more than the tears which they shed at his obsequies, manifested the greatness of their loss.

SIEGE OF PLATÆA (430–427).—The most memorable event of the years 430–427 was the siege
of Platæa, one of the most famous of antiquity,
on account of the stupendous efforts on both sides.
Five hundred men sustained during three years
the attacks of a numerous army of Lacedæmonians. After this stubborn resistance the Platæan
soldiers, having consumed all their provisions and
despairing of aid from Athens, formed the bold
resolution of making their escape through the
camp of the enemy. A portion of them, however, terrified at the danger, lost courage; the
others persisted in their design, and, availing
themselves of a dark and stormy night, forced a
passage and escaped ere the enemy could recover
from their surprise.

Those who had remained in Platæa surrendered on condition that their lives should not be
forfeited without a legal trial. Five Spartans
were appointed judges in the case. Without
charging the prisoners with any crime, the judges
simply asked whether they had during the present war rendered any service to the Lacedæmo-

nians or their allies. This question surprised and
perplexed the Platæans, and they reminded their
judges of the signal services they had rendered
to all Greece at the time of the Persian invasion.
But the fate of these brave, unhappy men was
already sealed. They were again asked whether,
since the beginning of the war, they had rendered
the Lacedæmonians any service, and the answer
being in the negative, they were slain without
mercy.

TREATY OF PEACE BROKEN BY ALCIBIADES
(421).—The cruel war had already lasted ten
years when the Athenians and Lacedæmonians,
equally weakened by losses, made a treaty of
peace which suspended for some time the animosity of the rival parties. After a year of
tranquillity the Peloponnesian war was rekindled with great fury (420). This rupture was
occasioned by Alcibiades, a young Athenian, a
rich, talented, and spirited youth. The flexi-
bility of his temper rendered him equally sus-
ceptible to the various impressions of virtue and
vice. He was a friend of Socrates. His inti-
macy with that celebrated philosopher was one
of the most remarkable circumstances of his
life.*

* Alcibiades prided himself especially on his riches, which con
sisted of vast domains. Socrates, one day showing him a map, asked
him to point out Attica: Alcibiades doing so without difficulty, was
requested to point out the part occupied by his domains. "They are
too inconsiderable," said he, "to be marked in so small a space."

Alcibiades was not born for repose, and, thirsting for honors, prevailed on the Athenians to break the treaty, hoping to distinguish himself, though replunging his country in the horrors of war. Many doubted the wisdom of complying with his wilful humor, but the mass, less clear-sighted, perceived in him only dazzling qualities, being blinded to the disorders of his private life. Abandoning themselves to the conduct of this ambitious youth, Alcibiades was enabled to prevail upon them to engage in a war with the Lacedæmonians, and at the same time advance with hostile intent against Syracuse in Sicily.

EXPEDITION OF ALCIBIADES INTO SICILY (415).—Syracuse, built by the Corinthians, was one of the most powerful and flourishing cities of the ancient world. After being the prey of many revolutions she settled on a republican form of government. During the Peloponnesian war a dispute arose between Syracuse and Segestes, a neighboring city. The latter, too feeble to oppose so powerful a rival, implored the aid of the Athenians. Athens considered this a favorable opportunity to achieve by the conquest of Syracuse that of Sicily. She made immense preparations, and soon her fleet departed from the Piræus, commanded by Alcibiades, Nicias,- and Lamachus.

"Behold," replied Socrates, "how proud an imperceptible spot of earth makes you."

Landing on the coast of Sicily, Alcibiades took the city of Catana by surprise. This was his first and last exploit during the Sicilian expedition, for an order came recalling him to Athens, where he had been accused, some days before the departure of the fleet, of mutilating the statues of Mercury. Alcibiades obeyed, and departed immediately; but reflecting during his voyage upon the fickleness of his fellow-citizens, and apprehensive that he would not be acquitted, he determined to deceive those who accompanied him and make his escape. He executed this design with his usual ingenuity. Having afterwards learned that the Athenians had condemned him to death as an outlaw, "I will let them know," he said, "that I am still alive." In fact, he joined the Lacedæmonians, and gained their favor by important advice calculated to injure his country.

SIEGE OF SYRACUSE; DEFEAT OF THE ATHENIAN ARMY (413).—Meanwhile Nicias, who after the departure of Alcibiades had the chief command, approached Syracuse, and blockading it by sea, he also nearly surrounded it on land by a line of intrenchments and redoubts. The Syracusans, closely pressed, were on the point of surrendering, when the arrival of Gylippus, a Spartan general, changed the aspect of affairs. He commenced by offering Nicias five days to depart from Sicily. Nicias scorned to answer

—✠—

such a proposal. Both sides prepared for battle. Gylippus first stormed and carried a fort near the city. This success enabled him to fortify Syracuse by extending the defenses beyond the wall of circumvallation, which would give the besieged a great advantage. Nicias endeavored to prevent the Spartans from building the ramparts, but failing, sent for aid to Athens.

Demosthenes was sent with an army almost as numerous as the first. His arrival reanimated the hopes of the besiegers and disheartened the besieged. But Demosthenes, wishing to signalize his arrival by some daring exploit, attempted during the night an ill-concerted attack, when his troops, seized with a sudden panic, threw down their arms and fled in confusion. The Athenians might still have safely retreated, but an eclipse of the moon occurring about this time, which they regarded as a bad omen, they postponed their departure till the next full moon, and this delay caused their ruin. The Syracusans, penetrating their designs, so entangled the retreating army that it was forced to surrender. Nicias, likewise, after a brave resistance, was forced to surrender himself a prisoner of war.

The Syracusans treated their captives with the utmost rigor. Both Nicias and Demosthenes were condemned to death, contrary to the intentions and promise of Gylippus. Seven thou-

———✦———

sand soldiers were thrown into dungeons, where they suffered indescribable torments, most of them perishing from hunger, thirst, and hardships. Some of them owed their preservation to the verses of Euripides, with the recital of which they charmed the ears of their conquerors. These liberated captives were wont on their return to hail Euripides as their deliverer.

RECALL AND SECOND EXILE OF ALCIBIADES. —The Athenians, dismayed by their losses, recalled Alcibiades as the only man really able to retrieve their fortunes. He eagerly acceded to the proposal, but not being willing to return except as a conqueror, first joined the Athenian fleet near the Asiatic coast and conquered the Lacedæmonians in two great battles, their admiral being slain and their army almost entirely destroyed (408). He then returned to Athens, where his arrival with the victorious fleet was hailed with every demonstration of joy (407). But his popularity was only transitory. Antiochus, one of his lieutenants, took occasion during his absence to attack the Lacedæmonians, who defeated him and captured fifteen galleys (406). The Athenians blamed Alcibiades for this loss, and he was again deprived of the command of the fleet and ten generals appointed in his place.

BATTLE NEAR THE ARGINUSÆ ISLANDS; INCONSTANCY OF THE ATHENIANS.—Athens, to repair her losses, made a last effort. She equipped one hundred and fifty vessels. The Spartans were under the command of Callicratidas, remarkable for his magnanimity and valor as well as for his great sensitiveness on the point of honor. Being advised not to hazard a battle against the superior numbers of the enemy, he replied that he could not avoid it without shame "Sparta," said he, "depends not upon a single man." The engagement took place near the Arginusæ. After incredible efforts of valor his vessel was overpowered, Callicratidas fell pierced with many wounds, and his death resulted in the total destruction of his fleet (406).

It was held a sacred duty among the ancients to bury their soldiers slain in battle. The Athenians had not only intended, but even taken measures to comply with this duty; but a violent storm prevented them from fulfilling their design. When the people at Athens heard that their dead had not been buried, they were so much incensed that they deposed their victorious generals and, without listening to their defence, condemned them to death. Among the thirty thousand citizens who composed the assembly, Socrates alone dared to protest against this unjust proceeding. The sentence was no sooner executed than the people themselves were filled with remorse, but their repentance came too tardily.

VICTORY OF LYSANDER AT ÆGOS POTAMOS (405).—Meanwhile the Lacedæmonians gave the command of their fleet to Lysander, a general as able as valiant. The Athenians met him at the Hellespont, and offered him battle near the mouth of a small river called Ægos Potamos. For four days they invited Lysander to battle, but the Lacedæmonians remained motionless. They waited on the fifth day till the Athenians had returned to their station, and the soldiers had, as usual, scattered themselves on shore. Lysander at that moment bore down upon them with his fleet, captured the empty ships, sent detachments to cut to pieces or disperse the troops on shore, and took three thousand prisoners with their generals. This masterly stroke was achieved in the space of an hour, yet was sufficient to prostrate the whole force of the Athenians and put an end to the Peloponnesian war, which had lasted twenty-seven years.

TAKING OF ATHENS (404).—In consequence the Athenians, without troops, vessels, provisions, or other resources, were compelled to surrender their ports to Lysander and his victorious army and to sue for peace. The Thebans and Corinthians advised that Athens be entirely demolished, but the Lacedæmonians declared they could not destroy a city which had formerly rendered such great service to Greece. Peace was therefore concluded upon the following conditions: the principal fortifications of the Piræus to be demolished; the Athenians to deliver up all their ships except twelve, to confine themselves within the limits of Attica, and in war to follow the Lacedæmonians wherever they wished to lead them.

ARTAXERXES II. (404–362); CYRUS THE YOUNGER; BATTLE OF CUNAXA (401).—After the death of Artaxerxes Longimanus, and of two other kings who reigned but a short time, the throne of Persia was occupied by their brother, Darius Nothus (424). The prominent features of this reign were an almost continual series of intrigues at court and revolts in the provinces, especially in Egypt, which at no time could brook the Persian yoke. Artaxerxes II., surnamed Mnemon on account of his extraordinary memory, succeeded Nothus towards the end of the Peloponnesian war.

He had a brother, Cyrus the Younger, who was intrusted with the government of Asia Minor. Not satisfied with this, the ambitious Cyrus aspired to the crown of his brother. With this view he raised an army of one hundred thousand barbarians and thirteen thousand Greeks, and at their head marched from Sardis towards Susa, resolved to deprive his brother of his crown and life. Artaxerxes, on his part, mustered a force of nine hundred thousand men and advanced against the rebel. The two armies met

—✝—

at Cunaxa, in Babylonia. In the midst of the conflict Cyrus, perceiving his brother, pushed towards him, slaying or putting to flight all who opposed his passage. Approaching Artaxerxes, he wounded him severely, but was himself wounded by the king and nobles, and fell dead at their feet.

Meanwhile the Greeks, attacking the host of barbarians to which they were opposed, threw them in such complete disorder that the king was unable to lead them back to the fight. The Greeks were completely victorious, but their young prince having fallen, they endeavored to make a hasty retreat towards their own country. Tissaphernes, general of Artaxerxes, not daring to attack them by force, used perfidy. He ensnared their chief officers and put them to death.

RETREAT OF THE TEN THOUSAND (401–400).— The Greeks, deprived of their generals, were in great consternation. They were nearly fifteen hundred miles from Greece, hemmed in by deep rivers and surrounded by enemies, without guides and without provisions. Xenophon revived their drooping courage and persuaded them to proceed on their march, after appointing new leaders. Himself and four others were appointed to this office. The Greeks committed themselves to their guidance, and set out fully determined to force their way through the enemy. Xenophon formed them in two columns, with the baggage enclosed therein. For want of vessels it was necessary to march to the mountains of Armenia, where the Tigris and Euphrates take their rise.

During the march they were harassed either by the Persians, who pursued them, or by the inhabitants of the country through which they passed. Other obstacles impeded their progress, such as deep, rapid streams, mountains and defiles and desert places, added to which were hunger and thirst, rain, cold, and snow sometimes to the depth of five or six feet. The Greeks, by their patience, constancy, and valor overcame all these difficulties, and in about seven months reached the Hellespont. The retreat of the ten thousand has always been considered a matchless feat in the art of warfare ; indeed, no enterprise could have been conceived with more boldness and valor, or conducted with greater success. Henceforward the Greeks looked forward with well-founded hope to the time when they would be able to overthrow the Persian empire.

VIRTUES OF SOCRATES ; THE THIRTY TYRANTS (404).—While the ten thousand under the guidance of Xenophon were traversing Asia with so much glory, Socrates, at Athens, succumbed under the united efforts of his enemies. This illustrious philosopher, perhaps the most accomplished man of pagan antiquity, was accustomed from childhood to a sober, laborious life.* It would be difficult to surpass him in his contempt for riches. Seeing one day a quantity of jewels and valuable merchandise, "How many things," said he, congratulating himself, "there are of which I have no need." Socrates loved poverty, but did not blush' to make known his wants. "If I had some money," said he one day to his friends, "I would buy a cloak." It became a matter of dispute among them who should make him this trifling present. His dominant virtues were tranquillity of soul and unfailing patience. At home he needed to exercise the latter. Xantippe, his wife, put it to the proof by her capricious, passionate disposition. One day, having vented upon him all the reproaches her fury could suggest, she dashed some foul water upon Socrates' head, at which he only laughed, saying, "So much thunder must needs produce a shower."

Socrates showed himself no less courageous during the many revolutions that agitated his country. Lysander, after the surrender of Athens, established there a council of thirty citizens. These magistrates soon became tyrants, who indulged in pillage and murder, opposed by no one. Socrates alone remained intrepid. He opposed their violent proceedings, consoled the

---

* We must not forget that Socrates was accused of inconstancy by his disciple Plato, of avarice by Cicero, and of pride and other vices by many of his contemporaries.

—✦—

afflicted, and labored to revive the hopes of the oppressed. He was a model of courage and firmness. The tyranny lasted for a period of eight months, when Thrasybulus, a citizen of rare merit, headed the bands of proscribed exiles and delivered his country from the hated tyrants' yoke.

INFLUENCE AND DEATH OF SOCRATES (400). — Socrates was most devoted to the instruction of youth. His was a philosophy of all times and places. He taught on every occasion—during his repasts, while walking, and in the army. Never had a philosopher more celebrated disciples. Plato and Xenophon alone would suffice to immortalize their master. The eagerness of the Athenian youths to follow him was wonderful. They left father and mother or abandoned parties of pleasure to listen to Socrates.

Socrates had enemies, but they were those who opposed the public good ; jealousy and hatred prompted their attacks. They charged him with introducing new gods and corrupting the Athenian youth. Socrates defended himself with the calm intrepidity of conscious innocence. But the judges were bribed; he was condemned, and he himself appointed to name his punishment. He answered : "Having spent my life in endeavors to serve my country and benefit my fellow-citizens, I deserve during the remainder of my days to be maintained at the expense of the republic." His judges, irritated, condemned him to drink hemlock. Socrates heard his sentence with perfect composure. One of his disciples began to express his grief at seeing him die innocent. "Why," replied Socrates, "would you have me die guilty?"

He drank the fatal hemlock and expired a few moments after (400). The Athenians soon repented their injustice. They not only punished his accusers but erected a splendid statue of brass in his honor, and revered him as a hero and demi-god. Socrates added to his moral virtues a belief in the immortality of the soul and in the providence of one God, creator and preserver of the universe. His fault was that he did not honor his God before the eyes of men, but to the last bent his knee to idols he knew so well were but folly and vanity.

PREPONDERANCE OF SPARTA; TREATY OF ANTALCIDAS (387).—Sparta was now at the height of prosperity. The Greeks of Asia Minor imploring her aid against the Persians, she sent them an army commanded by Agesilaus. This general, small of stature and deformed, but endowed with rare abilities, soon conquered Asia Minor, and caused the king of Persia himself to tremble. In order to arrest his progress, Artaxerxes distributed gold throughout Greece. Athens, Thebes, and Corinth soon formed a league against Sparta. Agesilaus, returning from Asia, defeated the allies at Coronea, in Bœotia (394); but the Lacedæmonian fleet was destroyed near Cnidus by Conon, one of the Athenian generals defeated at the battle of Ægos Potamos.

Conon, seconded by the fleet and gold of the persians, rebuilt in a few days the walls of Athens. The Lacedæmonians, alarmed at the increasing prosperity of Athens, commissioned Antalcidas to sign a humiliating treaty; all the Greek cities in Asia remained in possession of the king, and Sparta gave liberty to all the cities of Greece. This movement placed the ambitious republic in a position where she might dictate more imperiously than ever the laws to all Greece.

PELOPIDAS AND EPAMINONDAS; FREEDOM OF THEBES (378).—Sparta, not content with the power she already possessed, thought to increase it by the fraudulent occupation of the citadel of Thebes (382). This injustice caused Sparta's downfall, and it was Thebes herself that inflicted the blow that weakened her power. Thebes possessed at that time two men of uncommon merit —Pelopidas and Epaminondas. The first, who was still young and the only heir of an opulent family, spent his fortune in assisting the needy and distressed, showing by this noble conduct that he was not the slave but the true master of his riches. The second, through choice, lived in honorable poverty. He was at the same time

---

grave, magnanimous, prudent, and so much attached to truth that he would not utter a falsehood even in jest. Such were the two men who not only delivered Thebes from oppression, but raised it to the first rank among the cities of Greece.

Pelopidas, one of those whom the Lacedæmonian party had driven from Thebes, impressed upon his countrymen the necessity of a bold effort to free their oppressed country. All readily assented to his proposal. They set out with him, and, having entered Thebes at dusk and in disguise, marched towards the house where the magistrates appointed by Sparta were partaking of a banquet.

A few moments before the conspirators arrived a messenger came, bringing letters that contained a circumstantial account of the affair. This messenger had been directed to tell the magistrates that the contents of the letters were of a serious nature. " Serious affairs to-morrow,". exclaimed the first; and both himself and his guests continued to eat to excess. It was no difficult task for the assailants who surprised them in that state to put them to the sword. The following day Pelopidas besieged the citadel, and obliged the Lacedæmonian garrison to capitulate before assistance could be received. Scarcely had the place been evacuated when the expected succor arrived; but it was too late, and Thebes was now ready to make Sparta pay the penalty of her injustice.

BATTLE OF LEUCTRA (371).—After several campaigns, which proved the increasing superiority of Thebes, the Lacedæmonians, wishing to make a last effort, sent Cleombrotus, one of their kings, with twenty-four thousand men to ravage Bœotia. Epaminondas, then the general of the Thebans, marched against the enemy with only six thousand men, and engaged them near Leuctra (371). The combat was most obstinate. So long as Cleombrotus fought the victory remained doubtful; when he fell the Lacedæmonians, unable any longer to resist, were compelled to retire. Although they succeeded by prodigies of valor in carrying off the body of their leader, they could not succeed in retrieving the combat.

Epaminondas, in concert with Pelopidas, wishing to profit by this victory, re-established the Messenians in their country and invaded Laconia, which was pillaged and ravaged. Agesilaus, king of Sparta, being shut up within the confines of Lacedæmon, had the bitter mortification to see all the surrounding country overrun by the Thebans, and to witness with his own eyes the refutation of what he had frequently said, that "no Spartan woman had ever seen the smoke of an enemy's camp."

TRIAL OF PELOPIDAS AND EPAMINONDAS.— When the generals of the Theban army returned from their brilliant campaign, they were arraigned before a high court and tried for having kept the command of the troops a little longer than they were permitted by law. Pelopidas did not defend himself with his ordinary courage and intrepidity; hence he was with difficulty acquitted. Epaminondas acted in a very different manner. Instead of stooping to an apology for the great things he had done, he began to extol them in a strain of animated eloquence, saying that he would die with pleasure if it should be stated in the verdict against him that to him only was due the honor of the expedition against Sparta, and that it was an enterprise of their chief and without their consent. All the votes were in his favor, and he returned from his trial, as he was accustomed to return from battle, with additional glory and universal applause.

BATTLE OF MANTINEA (363).—The embers of war which, by the intervention of the Persian king, had been partly smothered, were rekindled after a few years with additional violence. The Thebans had Epaminondas for their general. He entered the hostile territory and prepared to besiege Mantinea. Being informed that Agesilaus was coming to the relief of that place, he conceived the idea of surprising Sparta, and immediately advanced toward it by a road different from that taken by Agesilaus. He would undoubtedly have taken the place in its defenceless state had not Agesilaus, forewarned, hastened to retrace his steps and reached the city before Epaminondas. The latter, finding himself baffled in this attempt, returned towards Mantinea. The Spartans followed, and both parties began to prepare for battle.

The troops on each side fought with undaunted bravery, but the Thebans, guided and animated by their intrepid general, at length forced the enemy to retire. At this decisive moment Epaminondas received a mortal wound. He was carried into camp, and the surgeons declared that he would expire as soon as the dart was extracted. When he was informed of the result of the battle and assured that the Thebans were completely victorious, he said to his friends: "All honor to the gods. I leave Thebes triumphant, proud Sparta humbled, and Greece delivered from the yoke of servitude. As to the rest, I do not look on myself as dying without issue. Leuctra and Mantinea are two illustrious daughters, who will keep my name alive." Having thus spoken, he drew the javelin from the wound and immediately expired (363). But one year before Pelopidas had fallen in the arms of victory. The power of Thebes began with two great men; it ended with them. After their death that city made peace with the Lacedæmonians and relapsed into its former obscurity.

REVIEW QUESTIONS.

From whom were the Greeks descended ? What can you say of the Pelasgi ? The Hellenes ? The Achæans ? The Æolians ? What of the Ionians and Dorians ? Who arrived in Greece between the years 1600 and 1300 B.C. ? In what did they instruct the people ? Name the four chief events of the heroic age. Describe them. What is meant by the "return of the Heraclidæ" ? Why did Codrus resolve to sacrifice himself ? Who was Lycurgus ? What proposal was made to him, and how did he receive it ? How did he secure obedience to his laws ? In whom was the chief authority vested ? Who were the Helots ? How did Lycurgus divide the land ? What currency did he introduce ? Why did he establish public repasts ? What did he enact in regard to the children of Sparta ? Describe his system of education. Why did the constitution of Lycurgus deserve censure rather than praise ? What was the condition of the Helots ? Why did the Spartans invade Messenia ? What can you say of Aristodemus ? Of Aristomenes ? Who was Tyrteus ? Name the seven sages of Greece. In what respect did the laws of Draco differ from those of Solon ? What was the Areopagus ? Describe the stratagem of Pisistratus. How did he exercise the power thus acquired ? What is he said to have made ? By whom was he succeeded ? What of Harmodius and Aristogiton ? What was ostracism ? What form of religious belief prevailed among the Greeks ? Their most famous festival ? Their most celebrated oracle ? Illustrate a characteristic feature of these oracles. Describe the Amphictyonic Council. Name the Grecian games. Of what did they consist ? How were the athletes trained ? How was the victor honored ? What was the origin of the Median wars ? How did the Athenians treat the ambassadors of Darius ? Describe the battle of Marathon. Who next invaded Greece ? What instances can you give of his great folly. What can you say of Leonidas and Thermopylæ ? Describe the battle of Salamis. How did Artemesia distinguish herself ? Describe the battle of Platæa. Of Mycale. How did Themistocles outwit

—✠—

the Lacedæmonians ? Why was Aristides more honored ? What was the end of Themistocles ? Who was Cimon ? What of his victories ? Who was Pericles ? By whom was the age of Pericles made famous ? What led to the Peloponnesian war? Who declared war against Athens? By whom was Attica attacked ? How did the Athenians resist the invaders ? Describe the plague at Athens. The death of Pericles. The siege of Platæa. In what year was peace made ? What led to the second war ? Describe the character of Alcibiades. The invasion of Sicily. Why was Alcibiades recalled? Why did he not return to Athens ? Describe the operations of Nicias. Of Demosthenes. How were the Athenian prisoners treated ? What caused the second banishment of Alcibiades. What can you say of Callicratidas ? Of Socrates ? Describe the victory of Lysander. What followed ? On what conditions was peace concluded ? How long did the first war last ? The second? Describe the "Retreat of the Ten Thousand." What was the character of Socrates. Describe his life. His death. By whom was a league formed against Sparta ? What more particularly led to her downfall? What of Pelopidas ? Of Epaminondas ? How were the Spartans expelled from Thebes ? Describe the battle of Leuctra. The trials of Pelopidas and Epaminondas. The battle of Mantinea. The death of Epaminondas.

CHAPTER VI.

MACEDONIA: EMPIRE OF ALEXANDER THE GREAT.

THE history of Macedonia, from the time when it is blended with Grecian history, comprises three periods: 1st. The foundation of the Macedonian greatness by Philip; 2d. The conquests and empire of Alexander the Great; 3d. The dismemberment of that empire.

Sec. 1. PHILIP (360–337 B.C.); *First Sacred War (355–345 B.C.); Second Sacred War; Battle of Chæronea (338 B.C.)*

PHILIP, KING OF MACEDONIA (360–336); HIS POLICY.—While the Grecian states sought to weaken each other by their endless wars, a power was arising in the East destined to have great influence on the civilized world. The kingdom of Macedonia was an hereditary kingdom situated to the north of Greece, and had been founded by the Corinthians nearly eight hundred years B.C. Its history offers nothing remarkable until the reign of Philip, a disciple of Epaminondas and father of Alexander the Great. This prince lifted Macedonia from its former obscurity, and succeeded within a few years in raising it to a marked pre-eminence over the neighboring nations. (The means which he employed for this purpose were not always honorable ; his usual arms were cunning and bribery. He considered no fortress impregnable that might be reached by a mule laden with gold ; in short, his whole life was a series of frauds, perfidy, and treachery. Such is the name he has left behind him, though he undoubtedly possessed some great qualities.

BIRTH OF ALEXANDER (356) ; PHILIP LOSES AN EYE.---Philip highly esteemed learned men and knew well the importance of education. He gave a striking proof of this at the birth of his son, Alexander the Great.* This prince being born at Pella, capital of Macedonia, his father chose the celebrated Aristotle as his son's preceptor, and wrote to him the following : "I inform you that Heaven has favored me with the birth of a son. I return thanks to the gods not so much for having given him to me as for having given him during the life of Aristotle ; I can justly promise myself that you will render

---

* Philip received three joyful messages on the same day : the first, that Parmenio, one of his generals, had gained a signal victory over the Illyrians ; the second, that his race-horse had won the prize at the Olympian games ; the third, of the birth of his son. Terrified at such rare good-fortune, he cried : "Great Jupiter, in return for so much good send me some slight misfortune." That same night Herostratus, wishing to make his name famous, burnt the temple of Diana, one of the seven wonders of the world.

him a successor worthy of me, and a king worthy of Macedonia."

Some time after Philip lost an eye under very singular circumstances. Whilst he was engaged in the siege of Methone a man named Aster offered to serve as marksman in his army, saying that he could·bring down birds in their most rapid flight. "Very well," said Philip, "I will engage your services when I war against starlings." This answer deeply offended the archer, who, finding his way into the besieged city, shot an arrow on which was written, "To Philip's right eye," and which actually pierced the right eye of that prince. The king sent him back the same arrow with this inscription : "If Philip takes Methone, he will hang Aster"; and he kept his word.

SACRED WAR (355–345) ; INTERVENTION OF PHILIP.—The Phocians, who inhabited the territories adjacent to Delphi, cultivated certain lands that were consecrated to Apollo, which were thereby profaned. Immediately the neighboring people exclaimed against them as guilty of sacrilege ; some from a spirit of sincerity, others to cover their private vengeance with a specious pretext of religion. The affair was brought before the Amphictyonic council. The Phocians were pronounced sacrilegious and condemned to pay a heavy fine. This decision led to the Sacred War. All the Grecian nations engaged in the quarrel and sided with one or the other party.

(Philip alone remained neutral, caring little for the interests of Apollo, but much for his own.) He profited by the confusion to extend his frontiers and subject Thrace. This enterprise terminated, and the Greeks appearing to him sufficiently weakened, he declared himself against the Phocians, and, having secured all the passes of Thermopylæ, he entered their country. The Phocians were easily conquered, and Philip obtained for himself all the honor and fruit of a war in which he had run no risks.

SECOND SACRED WAR (338); DEMOSTHENES (385–322).—Philip, master of Thermopylæ, the key of Greece, carried his schemes still farther. Under pretext of avenging the injury done to Apollo, he attacked and took Elatea, the most important city of Phocis (338).) The news of this conquest spread consternation to Athens and Thebes, which found themselves exposed to the attacks of this ambitious prince. In fact, he would have made of them an easy conquest had it not been for one who, with no weapon save his eloquence, endeavored to defend public liberty. This was Demosthenes.)

This celebrated man gave no early proofs of the extraordinary talents he possessed. Having at an early age lost his father and mother, he fell into the hands of dishonest guardians, who wasted his patrimony, thus impeding the youth's education by want of sufficient means; but he availed himself of every opportunity for the study of Plato and other masters, and is said to have ten times copied the orations scattered through the history of Thucydides, for the purpose of improving his style. The first time he attempted to speak in public his stammering voice, imperfect respiration, ungraceful gestures, and ill-arranged periods brought upon him general ridicule. This ill-success only served to show him what he lacked, and he determined to acquire a more perfect delivery. To cure himself of stammering he spoke with small pebbles in his mouth; to deepen his respiration he repeated verses in a loud voice while mounting steep or difficult places. He repaired to the sea-shore, and, whilst the waves were most violently agitated, declaimed aloud, in order to thus accustom himself to the cries and tumults of public assemblies. He studied gesticulation before a mirror. His labors were well repaid, for he carried the art of oratory to the highest degree of perfection, and all Greece hastened to hear Demosthenes.

This great man, as skilful and politic as he was eloquent, proved more hurtful to Philip than all the armies and fleets of the Athenians. As soon as he penetrated that king's ambitious designs he unceasingly combated them in his celebrated orations known as the *Philippics* and *Olynthiacs.*

BATTLE OF CHÆRÓNEA (338); DEATH OF PHILIP (336).—No sooner was the loss of Elatea known than Demosthenes prevailed upon the Athenians and Thebans to forget former animosities and unite for their common defence.*

Philip, not being able by diplomacy to prevent this league, determined to crush it. He entered the Bœotian territory and met the confederates near Chæronea (338). Himself taking command of the right wing, he gave the left to his son Alexander, then a youth of seventeen years. The battle raged with great fury, one army fighting to maintain its supremacy, the other to preserve its freedom. Alexander, after a long resistance, broke the ranks of the sacred band, which was the flower of the Theban army.

Philip for some time was less successful. Part of his troops began to waver, and the 'Athenians, believing themselves already successful, cried out: "Come, let us pursue them into Macedo-

---

* During the same year (338) Demosthenes expended part of his fortune to rebuild the walls of Athens. Ctesiphon proposed to give him a crown of gold as a recompense. Æschines opposed this as contrary to law. It was on this occasion the two greatest orators of Greece arrayed against each other all the powers of eloquence. Æschines lost his cause and was banished. Passing to the isle of Rhodes, he opened there a school of eloquence. His pupils greatly admired his own production, but when they heard the oration of Demosthenes the plaudits were redoubled. "What applause," said Æschines, "would you not have bestowed had you heard Demosthenes himself deliver this oration!"

—✠—

nia." The king, seeing the enemy eager in the pursuit of some fugitives instead of attacking his main body in the flank, calmly said: "The Athenians know not how to conquer." Immediately he commanded his phalanx to wheel about, and, attacking his foes in flank and rear, threw them in disorder and inflicted upon them a total defeat.

(Philip made a generous use of his victory. He granted peace to the two republics, and was named by them commander-in-chief of their forces against Persia.) For a long time he contemplated the conquest of Asia, but death surprised him in the midst of his vast preparations. An act of injustice cost him his life. A young Macedonian lord had been grossly insulted by a favorite of Philip. That prince refusing to give satisfaction, the young man in a paroxysm of fury stabbed him during the celebration of some festivity.)

Sec. 2. ALEXANDER THE GREAT (336–323 B.C.): *Submission of Greece; Conquests in Asia; Ruin of the Persian Empire.*

TAKING AND RUIN OF THEBES (335).—Alexander was but twenty years of age when he ascended the throne of Macedonia. All the barbarians were endeavoring to throw off the yoke imposed by the late king. The Greeks espe-

—✦—

cially, animated by the eloquence of Demosthenes, formed a powerful league against the new
king. Deceived by his youth, they spoke of
him as a child who needed to be chastised. Alexander hastened to prove his manhood. Placing
himself at the head of his army, he surprised
Thebes, and, having defeated the Thebans with
great slaughter, levelled their city to the ground.

This example of severity terrified all the neighboring cities, especially the Athenians. They
hastened to make their submission, and were
happy to obtain peace under moderate conditions. In Corinth Alexander was proclaimed
commander-in-chief of the Greek forces. Having
received the congratulations of many distinguished persons, he went to see the Cynic Diogenes, celebrated for his contempt of riches.
The king, finding the Cynic lying in the sun,
asked him if he could render him any service.
"Stand from between me and the sun," said
Diogenes. The young king said to his friends:
"I would wish to be Diogenes, were I not Alexander."

BATTLE OF GRANICUS (334).—Alexander, having arranged affairs in Macedonia, soon after set
out for Asia, and passed the Hellespont without
difficulty.* Arrived at the banks of the Grani-

* Landing near the ruins of Troy, he caused games to be celebrated
around the tomb of Achilles. "Happy Achilles!" cried he, "having
had Patroclus as a friend and Homer to sing thy exploits." Alexan-

cus, in Phrygia, he found a hostile force of one hundred thousand men ready to dispute its passage. Nothing daunted, Alexander plunged into the stream, followed by his troops. It was a perilous attempt, and Alexander's life was in danger. A battle-axe was about to descend with deadly stroke upon his head, when Clitus, one of his officers, saved his life by cutting off the hand of the Persian. The enemy, losing their general, were soon defeated, dispersed, and Alexander was left master of the country (334). The victorious prince hastened over Lesser Asia,* taking Ephesus, Sardis, Magnesia, Miletus, Halicarnassus, finally reaching Tarsus, in Cilicia, on the banks of the Cydnus.

ILLNESS AND MAGNANIMITY OF ALEXANDER —At sight of the limpid waters of the Cydnus, Alexander, covered with dust and sweat, desired to bathe. No sooner had he plunged in than he was benumbed with cold and carried back half dead to his tent. Aware of the approach of Persian army under command of Darius, Alex-

---

der greatly admired the *Iliad*. He knew it entirely by heart, and carried it with him in a precious casket. Next to Homer he admired Pindar most. He spared the house of that poet in the destruction of Thebes.

* Arriving at Gordium, in Asia Minor, he heard an ancient tradition that he who could untie the Gordian knot would become master of Asia. It was a knot which Gordius, a king, had tied on the yoke of his chariot. Alexander, not being able to untie it, cut it with his sword, and thus persuaded his soldiers that he would accomplish the oracle.

by the eloquence of De

powerful league against t

d by his youth, they s

who needed to be chasti

ed to prove his manhood.

head of his army, he

aving defeated the Th

, levelled their city to

of severity terrified al

especially the Athe

ake their submissio

in peace under m

rinth Alexander

chief of the Greek

—✣—

army numbered no more than forty thousand. But the Persian monarch would not listen to this salutary advice, and advanced as far as the small town of Issus. The spot could not have been more disadvantageous for him, nor more advantageous for Alexander, who, being protected on one side by the sea and on the other by the mountains, was in no danger of being surrounded.

Hence the issue of the battle was not long uncertain between a confused multitude and a well-disciplined army. Alexander, having broken the left wing of the Persians, where Darius was stationed, next attacked the centre, and then the right, defeating both. His victory was complete. The enemy lost more than one hundred thousand men, their camp was taken, and among the captives was Sisygambis, the mother of Darius, with his wife, two daughters, and a son yet a child. Alexander treated them with the utmost courtesy and respect, and saluted Sisygambis with the title of mother and granted her many favors. On the death of Alexander she is said to have expired with grief. If Alexander had always acted in this manner he would justly have merited the title of Great. He bore his first triumphs with a moderation and wisdom that placed him among the best of men, but at length he became proud and arrogant, giving full rein to his basest passions.

——✠——

TAKING OF TYRE (332) ; ALEXANDER AT JE-
RUSALEM.—Alexander, victor of Issus, continued
his march towards Syria and Phœnicia. Every
city opened its gates, save Tyre. That city,
destroyed by Nabuchodonosor, had been rebuilt
on an island close to the continent. Her commerce and riches caused her to be named the
Queen of the Sea. Proud of her advantages, she
dared refuse Alexander entry within her walls.
The young conqueror, affronted by her refusal,
determined to besiege Tyre, which he took after
seven months of incredible hardships. All the
inhabitants were either put to the sword or sold.

Alexander, piqued at the attachment of the
Jews to the Persian king, marched against Jerusalem, determined to inflict on it the severest
punishments. But God, who holds in his hand
the hearts of princes, suddenly changed that of
Alexander. He recognized in the high-priest
Jaddus the venerable personage who had appeared to him in his sleep while he was in Macedonia, and had promised him the conquest of
Asia. Filled with respect, he prostrated himself before the priest of the true God, and, in
place of ill-treating the Jews, loaded them with
benefits.

ALEXANDER IN EGYPT AND AT THE TEMPLE
OF JUPITER-AMMON.—Alexander then advanced
towards Egypt. The Egyptians, tired of the
Persian yoke, hastened to welcome him rather

than to offer opposition, and he was soon in quiet possession of the whole country. At this period, giving scope to the pride of his heart, he wished to pass for a god. Full of this extravagant idea, he proceeded across the Libyan sands to the temple of Jupiter-Ammon, where the priest, bribed by presents, declared him the son of Jupiter. The favorable situation of a part of the northern coast of Egypt induced him to build there a great city, which was called, after his own name, Alexandria.

BATTLE OF ARBELA (331).—When Alexander had sufficiently flattered his vanity he left Egypt and advanced towards the Euphrates and Tigris, which he crossed without opposition. Soon after he found himself in the presence of Darius with an immense army. The combat having begun, the Persians seemed at first to have the advantage. They captured the camp of the Macedonians and began to plunder it. Alexander, thinking victory would compensate every loss, was careful not to send succor there. Placing himself at the head of his men, he fell with fury on the enemy, and, penetrating to Darius, slew his charioteer. The Persians in the vicinity of Darius, believing their king was killed, were thrown into a panic. Darius himself, terrified at beholding Alexander so near, stripped off his royal garments, mounted his horse, and precipitately fled.

——✛——

Meanwhile, Parmenio, finding himself in im-
minent danger, sent word to Alexander, who,
desisting from the pursuit of the king, hastened
to protect his left wing ; but the danger was
past when he arrived. The Persians, dispirited
at the results of the engagement, fled. Such
was the battle of Arbela, which cost the Persians more than three hundred thousand men,
and which gave to the conqueror the empire of
Asia.

BURNING OF PERSEPOLIS.—Alexander, having
destroyed the enemy, marched to Babylon and
Susa, which opened their gates to him. Having
defeated an army under Ariobarzanes, he entered Persepolis, the capital of Persia, where he
found immense treasures, which he distributed
as rewards among his soldiers. It was at Persepolis, while at a party of pleasure, that a woman
who had been admitted to the feast said that it
would be a noble termination were they to burn
the palace of Xerxes, who had burned Athens.
The company, having drunk to excess, applaud-
ed this proposition, and it was Alexander himself who applied the first torch. When sober he
tried to extinguish the flames, but it was too
late ; the palace was entirely consumed with its
accumulated treasures.

DEATH OF DARIUS (330).—Darius fled as far
as Ecbatana, capital of Media. Alexander con-
tinuing to approach, he endeavored to retreat

still further, but Bessus, one of his generals, made himself master of his person and loaded him with fetters. When the traitor learned that the Macedonians were fast approaching he tried to force Darius to accompany him in his flight, but the king refusing to advance with his rebellious subject, Bessus, enraged, pierced him with arrows. Alexander arrived at the moment when this unfortunate prince had just expired. He wept bitterly and caused his funeral to be conducted with royal magnificence. With Darius ended the Persian Empire ; it had lasted two hundred and eight years, from the taking of Babylon by Cyrus. Shortly after Bessus paid the just forfeit of his crime. Having fallen into the hands of Alexander, he was condemned to be quartered. Afterwards encamping on the Jaxartes, Alexander built the city of Alexandreschata, so called as marking the limits of Alexander's Scythian expedition.

DEATH OF CLITUS (328).—Alexander, having no more enemies to conquer, abandoned himself entirely to pride, anger, luxury, and debauchery. In one of his orgies, having drunk immoderately, he began to extol his own exploits, and spoke contemptuously of those of his father, Philip. Clitus, the brother of the nurse of Alexander— the same who had saved his life when crossing the Granicus—defended Philip, and in the heat of the dispute forgot that he spoke to his king.

———✦———

Alexander, highly incensed, dissembled for a time his anger, but, waiting till Clitus was about to depart, struck him dead with his poignard. The king's anger being extinguished by the blood of his friend, he became a prey to the keenest remorse.

EXPEDITION INTO INDIA (327); KING PORUS. —As ambition was still his predominant passion, and as the Macedonians were discontented with his new manner of life, Alexander turned his attention toward the subjugation of India. After a march of sixteen days he arrived at the river Indus, from which the country takes its name. All the kings of the country except Porus came to make their submission. It was difficult to attack Porus, as the Hydaspes, a deep, broad, and rapid stream, separated the two kings, and Porus, with an immense army, defended the passage. Alexander, therefore, had recourse to stratagem. Making preparations as if to cross the river in a certain place, he passed over in another during a frightful storm, the very violence of which favored the prosecution of his designs. Porus, defeated and made prisoner, appeared before his conqueror, and, when asked how he wished to be treated, nobly answered, "Like a king." Alexander, moved by the noble bearing of the Indian prince, restored to him his kingdom and added to it several other provinces.

—✦—

MURMURS OF THE MACEDONIANS ; RETURN TO BABYLON (325).—Alexander wished to cross the Ganges, the largest river of India, to extend his conquests, but the discontent and entreaties of his army induced him to retrace his steps towards the west. Before leaving India for Babylon he had the satisfaction of viewing from the mouth of the Indus the vast expanse of ocean. During the long march through the deserts his army was tortured with famine and other hardships. Arriving in the fertile country of Babylon, he indulged in feasts for seven days, during which he never ceased to drink. Happily for the Macedonians, the conquered nations did not then endeavor to shake off their yoke. A thousand men would have sufficed to exterminate these conquerors of the world, buried in wine and debauchery.

PROJECTS AND DEATH OF ALEXANDER (323).—Alexander found in Babylon ambassadors from nearly all parts of the world, who had assembled to pay him homage. Meanwhile, his mind was occupied with new enterprises : the conquest of Arabia, the circumnavigation of Africa, a war against Carthage, and the subjugation of Europe. Death, however, did not permit him to execute any of these projects. At the close of a banquet, in which he drank to excess, he was seized with a violent fever, and in a few days was reduced to the last extremity. As a mark of affection he gave his hand to his soldiers' to kiss. Being asked whom he wished to succeed him, " The most worthy," was the reply. And they enquiring further when he wished them to pay him divine honors, he answered, " When you are happy." These were his last words, shortly after which he expired.*

CHARACTER OF ALEXANDER.—Critics have ever been divided in their judgment as to the true estimate of the character of Alexander. By some he is ranked as the first of heroes; by others it is thought that his great deeds are overshadowed by vanity, debauchery, and cruelty. His military talents were of the highest order; he overran and subdued the greater part of the world known to the ancients in an astonishingly short space of time. His views of public policy were liberal and enlightened, and he was a patron of arts and letters, his favorite book being the *Iliad.* Much of what was greatest and noblest in his character was due to the teachings of the illustrious Aristotle, and it is no small praise to say that Alexander was, at least in the early part of his career, every way worthy of such a teacher.

Alexander was also capable of great generosity

* At the death of Alexander his family comprised : Olympia, his mother ; Philip Aridæus, his brother ; Cleopatra and Thessalonica, his sisters ; Statira, daughter of Darius, and Roxana, his wives. Roxana shortly after the death of Alexander gave birth to a son, who, under the name of Alexander Ægus, was proclaimed king jointly with Philip, the brother of the late king.

and magnanimity, as was shown in his treatment of the family of Darius, and by his conduct in the scene with the physician Philip. With these virtues, too, he possessed great strength of intellect and will; but unhappily his passions were still stronger. Thus, we see him basely and foolishly seeking the flattery of being called a god; in a fit of rage murdering his friend and foster-brother; and in the midst of a drunken revelry applying the incendiary torch. Pope aptly terms him

"The youth who all things but himself subdued."

In personal appearance Alexander is said to have been of medium height, and with a countenance of great majesty. He excelled in martial exercises, and especially in horsemanship.

Sec. 3. DISMEMBERMENT OF THE EMPIRE OF ALEXANDER THE GREAT: *Anarchy of Twenty-two Years* (323–301 B.C.); *Antigonus and Demetrius; Battle of Ipsus* (301).

THE INHERITANCE AND HEIRS OF ALEXANDER THE GREAT.—No prince had ever left an empire so vast as that of Alexander. Its limits were, on the north, the Danube, the Euxine Sea, the Caucasian Mountains, the Caspian Sea, and Jaxartes; on the east, the Emodus Mountains, Hyphasis, and Indus; on the south, the Arabian Sea, the Persian Gulf, the deserts of Arabia, and the cataracts of Syene; on the west, Libya, the Mediterranean and Adriatic Seas. It was easier to conquer so many countries than to peacefully govern them. Alexander seems to have foreseen this when he refused to designate his successor, and when he predicted his would be bloody obsequies. His generals, indeed, during seven years endeavored each to obtain predominance over the others. Philip Aridæus, the brother of Alexander, though weak in mind, was chosen king, and associated with him was Alexander Ægus, the son of Roxana. Perdiccas, to whom Alexander when dying had given his ring, was appointed regent. The other generals, numbering thirty, divided among themselves as satrapies the provinces of the empire. Antipater took Macedonia and Greece; Ptolemy, Egypt; Antigonus, Lydia and other portions of Asia Minor; Lysimachus, Thrace; Eumenes, Cappadocia, etc.

ANARCHY; THE FIVE KINGS (306).—The death of Alexander was followed by a series of revolts, which his generals sternly quelled.*

---

* The most celebrated revolt was that of the Greeks, incited and encouraged by the eloquence of Demosthenes. The Athenians and their allies won the victory near Lamia, in Thessaly—whence the name of "Lamian War"—but they were cut to pieces by Antipater. Demosthenes, being resolved not to fall into the hands of the victors, determined to poison himself (322). Phocion, his rival in eloquence and his superior in virtue and courage, could not obtain his pardon from Antipater. Five years later Phocion, himself unjustly accused, was condemned to death, and while he drank the fatal hemlock he warned his son not to forget the ingratitude of the Athenians.

—◈—

But, as they thought more of satisfying their
ambition than preserving order, they began a
struggle among themselves which, marked by
treachery and other crimes, lasted twenty-two
years. To render each independent in his province, they at first formed a league against Perdiccas, who wished to maintain the unity of the
empire. The regent was about to give battle to
Ptolemy when he was murdered by his own soldiers while passing the Nile (321). His most
powerful enemy, Antipater, succeeded him, and
thus prevented the succession of Eumenes, the
only general truly attached to the royal family.
Antipater died shortly after, leaving the regency
to an old man, Polyperchon (319). Eumenes,
whose bravery equalled his fidelity, made heroic
efforts against the new regent. But he was betrayed by his own soldiers and delivered to Antigonus, who put him to death, although they
had formerly been allied in the closest friendship (316).

Antigonus, having become master of a great
part of Asia, took the title of king. His power,
added to his still greater pretensions, gave the
other generals just cause to fear that their provinces would not long remain in their possession.
They therefore leagued against him, each, following his example, taking the title of king ; Ptolemy in Egypt, Lysimachus in Thrace, Seleucus
in Babylon, and Cassander in Macedonia, which

—⧾—

he had occupied since the death of Antipater. As to the regent, he took refuge in Peloponnesus, where he had so little power that he has left no mark in history.

DEMETRIUS POLIORCETES ; SIEGE OF RHODES (304–303).—Antigonus made preparations to withstand his opponents. He was ably seconded by his son Demetrius, surnamed Poliorcetes ("taker of cities"). This young prince was remarkable for his noble appearance ; his natural vivacity was tempered by a heroic air and a majesty truly remarkable. When occupied in some military enterprise, he spoke and acted like a hero ; at other times he seemed the personification of effeminacy and luxury. This diversity of character appeared likewise in his fortunes and rendered his whole life an alternation of extraordinary prosperity or signal disaster. After several expeditions, which made him master of Athens and the isle of Cyprus, he advanced to the isle of Rhodes, whose inhabitants had refused to aid Ptolemy in the late war against the Egyptians.* The Rhodians were early noted for their commerce and skill in navigation. They courageously prepared to defend themselves. If the attack

---

* He drove from Athens (307) Demetrius of Phalern~, who had governed that city since the death of Phocion, in whose honor the Athenians erected three hundred and sixty statues of bronze. Demetrius, having retired to the court of Ptolemy, presided over the celebrated library of Alexandria and advised the translation of the Septuagint.

---

was vigorous, the resistance was not less so. Demetrius invented many formidable machines, but the besieged set them on fire during the night and destroyed the greater part. Demetrius invented new ones which were proof against fire, and among others an immense wooden tower which seemed to forbode the fall of the city. The besieged, not being able to burn it, had recourse to another expedient. They undermined the place over which the *keliopolis* (the name of the terrible machine) had to pass in its approach to the walls ; when it reached the spot the earth gave way beneath it, and the machine sank so deep that no exertion of the besiegers could again raise it. Demetrius, despairing of success, decided to retire. He entered into treaty with the Rhodians, and as a mark of esteem presented to them his war-machines. The Rhodians sold them and with the money erected the famous Colossus, between whose feet vessels had to pass when entering or leaving the harbor. Being overthrown by an earthquake, it lay on the ground until the seventh century, when the Saracens, having subdued the island of Cyprus, sold it to a Jewish merchant, who loaded with it 800 camels.

BATTLE OF IPSUS (301).—Demetrius, after raising the siege of Rhodes, joined Antigonus, and with him marched against the confederate armies commanded by Seleucus and Lysimachus.

The hostile armies met near the city of Ipsus in Phrygia. Demetrius fought with so much valor that he put the enemy to flight. But having, through a vain desire of glory, rashly continued the pursuit of the vanquished, he lost a victory which was already his. On his return he found the passage obstructed by the elephants of Seleucus. His infantry surrendered to the confederates, while a party rushed against Antigonus, who was vainly expecting the return of his son. The old king fought with desperate courage, but fell at last pierced with darts. The four allied princes, after this victory, distributed among themselves the dominions of Antigonus. Seleucus had for his share, under the name of Syria, nearly all of Asia to the river Indus. The empire of Alexander was thus divided into four kingdoms—namely, the kingdom of Thrace, which did not last long ; the kingdom of Macedon, that of Egypt, and that of Syria, which was the most powerful and considerable of the four.

REVIEW QUESTIONS.

When and by whom was the Kingdom of Macedonia founded? Who first made it powerful? What means did he employ? What three messages did Philip receive on a certain day? Repeat his letter to Aristotle. Relate an incident of the siege of Methone. What. led to the Sacred War? How did Philip act? Who aroused the people to a sense of their danger? What of the early efforts of Demosthenes? Their result? Describe the battle of Chæronea. Did Philip abuse his victory? Describe his death. By whom was Philip succeeded? How did Alexander signalize his accession to the throne? Describe the battle of the Granicus. What cities did he take in Asia Minor? Relate an anecdote of Alexander at Corinth. At Troy. At Gordium. What occurred at Tarsus on the Cydnus? Describe the battle of Issus. The siege of Tyre. Describe the march of Alexander against Jerusalem. His visit to the temple of Jupiter-Ammon. The battle of Arbela. What happened at Persepolis? Describe the death of Darius. Of Clitus. Who resisted Alexander in India? How did Alexander cross the Hydaspes? Describe the interview between him and Porus. Why did Alexander return to Babylon? What new enterprises did he contemplate? Describe the manner of his death. What was the extent of his empire? Who were his successors? What of Perdiccas? The other generals? Describe the revolt of the Greeks, and its result. What befell Perdiccas? Antipater? Eumenes? How did the five kings divide the empire? What can you say of Poliorcetes? Describe the siege of Rhodes. The battle of Ipsus. How was the empire of Alexander finally divided.

CHAPTER VII.

STATES FORMED FROM THE DISMEMBERMENT OF THE EMPIRE OF ALEXANDER.

THE principal states formed from the dismemberment of the empire of Alexander were the kingdoms of Egypt, Syria, and Macedonia. With the history of Macedonia mingles that of Greece. The kingdom of Thrace disappeared with Lysimachus.

Sec. 1. EGYPT UNDER THE LAGI (323–30 B.C.); *Glory and Prosperity under the three first Ptolemies (323–222 B.C.) ; Rivalry with Syria ; Anarchy and Intervention of the Romans.*

PTOLEMY I., SOTOR (323–285) ; WISDOM OF HIS GOVERNMENT.—Ptolemy I., surnamed Sotor,* reigned nearly forty years and founded the dynasty of the Lagi, so named from his father, Lagus. (Less ambitious than the other generals of Alexander, he warred only to defend his province of Egypt, to which he added Cyrenaica, the isle of Cyprus, and Phœnicia. He was the ablest as well as the best sovereign of his dynasty, and left examples of prudence and justice imi-

* Sotor—that is, "saviour." This name was bestowed upon him by the Rhodians in acknowledgment of the services which he rendered them.

tated by but few of his successors. His habits while upon the throne were marked by the plainness and modesty which ever characterized him; and when told that his dignity required greater pomp and splendor, he answered that a king should make his true greatness consist not in being rich himself but in enriching others. He loved the sciences, protected the learned, and began the library of Alexandria, famous for the choice and collection of its volumes, which amounted to seven hundred thousand.

PTOLEMY II., PHILADELPHUS (285–247); THE VERSION OF THE SEPTUAGINT.—Ptolemy II., surnamed Philadelphus,* inherited from his father a taste for the arts. He completed in the first year of his reign the building of the light-house of Pharos, one of the seven wonders of the world. It was a lofty tower of white marble, bearing on its summit a perpetual light to guide vessels approaching the shores of Egypt during the night. The king also made valuable additions to the library founded by his predecessor, and enriched it with a translation of the Old Testament from the Hebrew into Greek. The high-priest of the Jews sent him a copy of the books of Moses and other sacred books written in letters of gold, and seventy-two deputies to

* Philadelphus—that is, "lover of his brothers"—thus ironically surnamed because he had, under pretence of self-defence, put his two brothers to death.

translate them. They completed the version of the Old Testament known as the Septuagint. The king greatly admired the profound wisdom of the laws of Moses, and sent back the deputies with magnificent presents for themselves, for their high-priest, and for the Temple of Jerusalem.

CANAL BETWEEN THE RED SEA AND THE MEDITERRANEAN.—Ptolemy Philadelphus devoted his chief care to enriching his kingdom. He established, by means of a canal and the Nile, easy communication between the Red and Mediterranean Seas, thus placing nearly all the trade of the Oriental nations in the hands of his subjects, and rendering Alexandria the general emporium of the then known world. That city became pre-eminent as a seat of learning, science, and art, and was adorned with many edifices of great splendor. Its inhabitants were divided into three classes—the Egyptians, the mercenaries in the service of the king, and the *Alexandrians*, a name given to strangers who settled there, mostly Greeks and Jews.

PTOLEMY III., EUERGETES (247–222) ; EXPEDITION INTO SYRIA.—Ptolemy III., surnamed Euergetes—that is, "the beneficent"—had scarcely ascended the throne when he undertook to avenge the death of his sister Berenice, Queen of Syria, whom her rival Laodice had caused to be murdered. A powerful army, supported by numerous auxiliaries, enabled him to make the Syrian court feel all the weight of his indignation. He not only put Laodice to death, but overran the whole of Syria, which he conquered and ravaged even beyond the Euphrates. (The booty from this expedition reached the enormous sum of forty thousand talents (between forty and fifty millions of dollars). Passing through Jerusalem on his return, he offered many sacrifices to the true God in thanksgiving for his victory over the Syrians. He was the last prince of his dynasty that showed any virtue; his successors were monsters of wickedness and profligacy.)

PTOLEMY IV., PHILOPATOR (222–205) ; BATTLE OF RAPHIA.—Philopator,* son of Euergetes, prosecuted a war against Antiochus the Great, King of Syria, who wished to recover the provinces dismembered from his kingdom by Ptolemy III. After several expeditions, which were not decisive, the two kings met at Raphia. (Resolved to decide their quarrel, they fought desperately. Antiochus defeated the left wing of the Egyptians, but rashly continued the pursuit of the fugitives. Philopator meantime broke the left wing of the Syrians, and then attacked the centre before Antiochus could come to its aid. The victory rested with Philopator, who obtained peaceful possession of Palestine and a part of

* Philopator—"lover of his father"—so surnamed because he caused that parent to be poisoned,

———✦———

Syria) (Henceforward he gave himself up to debauchery and crime. Besides poisoning his father, he openly killed his wife and brother. His continued debauchery and intemperance caused his death in his thirty-seventh year)

PTOLEMY V., EPIPHANES (205–181), AND PTOLEMY VI., PHILOMETOR (181–146); THE RING OF POPILIUS.—(Ptolemy Epiphanes) or the "illustrious," succeeded Philopator. (He is known only by his perfidy and cruelty.) He was poisoned. Ptolemy Philometor,* his son, made war against Antiochus Epiphanes, who made himself master of all Egypt, and even captured Philometor and held him in confinement. The Egyptians, seeing their king in the hands of Antiochus, regarded him as lost, and placed on the throne his brother Ptolemy, surnamed Physcon on account of a protuberant abdomen. Antiochus, under pretence of re-establishing the deposed king, but really intending the conquest of the country, marched to Alexandria and besieged it. He would undoubtedly have taken the city had not an embassy been sent from Rome which defeated his plans.)

Popilius, one of the ambassadors, presenting him the senate's decree, enjoined him to read it and answer immediately. Antiochus, having read it, said he would deliberate with his friends.

---

* Philometor—"lover of his mother," whom he hated.

—✠—

Popilius, indignant that the king spoke of delay, drew with his rod a circle on the sand around Antiochus, and, raising his voice, said : "You must reply to the senate before you leave the circle which I have traced." The king, terrified at this order and having reflected a little, said that he would do what the senate demanded, and returned to Syria (168).

INGRATITUDE AND REIGN OF PTOLEMY VII., PHYSCON (146–117).—After the retreat of Antiochus the two Ptolemies resolved to make an equal division of their country. Philometor held Egypt and the isle of Cyprus; Libya and Cyrenaica fell to Physcon. But this arrangement was not of long duration. Physcon, ill-content with his part, and naturally an enemy of peace, quarrelled with Philometor and drove him from his states. But the latter soon returned, conquered Physcon in his turn, and made him prisoner. It was expected that he would take terrible vengeance on his unnatural brother. On the contrary, he pardoned everything and restored to him Libya and Cyrenaica (157). This generous act put an end to their hatred, and they ever after lived on good terms.

The death of Philometor left Physcon master of Egypt. He profited by this only to give himself up to the most frightful excesses, to which death only put an end (117).

PTOLEMY XI., AULETES (80–52) ; INTERVEN-

TION OF THE ROMANS.—After Physcon and two other kings scarcely better than he, Ptolemy Auletes—" the piper "—ascended the throne. The Egyptians had long been allies of the Roman people. Auletes aspired to the same title, but his surname rendered him contemptible at Rome. Cæsar and Pompey, already very powerful at Rome, sold him their protection, and, at the price of six hundred talents, he obtained the title of ally of Rome. Auletes, to cancel this debt, made such extraordinary levies that his incensed subjects obliged him to fly from Egypt. Some time after, however, he was re-established by a Roman army and put in full possession of his states. He now suspected of hostility every one who possessed riches, and seized their treasures. His subjects bore this without complaint, but a Roman soldier having killed a cat by mistake, neither the authority of the king nor the fear of the Roman armies hindered them from tearing the culprit to pieces for having outraged one of the gods of the country.

PTOLEMY XII., DENIS AND CLEOPATRA (52–48); POMPEY AND CÆSAR.—Auletes, dying, left the crown conjointly to his two children, Ptolemy and Cleopatra, and placed them under the care of the Roman people, particularly under Pompey, who was then the first citizen of the republic. Soon, however, ambition separated the brother and sister, and the latter was driven away.

About this time Pompey, defeated by Cæsar at Pharsalia, fled to Egypt, where he hoped to find refuge. He found there but death. Ptolemy, yielding to the advice of two infamous ministers, assassinated this great man at the moment when, relying on the hospitality of the Egyptian shore, he was about to land. Ptolemy believed that in so doing he would win the favor of Cæsar ; but he was deceived. Cæsar heard of the murder with indignation. Incensed at such base treason, and won by the flattery of Cleopatra, he replaced her on the throne. Ptolemy, ill-content with this proceeding, had recourse to arms, but was vanquished by Cæsar and perished in combat (48).

PTOLEMY XIII., THE CHILD (48–44), AND CLEOPATRA (48–30) ; ANTONY AND OCTAVIA.— Cæsar, master of Alexandria, obliged Cleopatra to reign conjointly with her young brother, Ptolemy XIII., "the Child." But Cleopatra, although only twenty-one years of age, had already committed every crime that would further her ambition, and, not wishing to share the throne with her brother, she poisoned him, and reigned alone in Egypt until she gained the heart of a Roman general, Mark Antony, who, to marry her, repudiated his wife, Octavia, sister to Cæsar Augustus. This marriage brought the Roman army into Egypt. Cleopatra betrayed and sacrificed Antony; but her perfidy could not save her, and, reduced to despair, she terminated by the bite of an asp a life that had been but a tissue of crimes. So ended the first kingdom of Egypt (30 B.C.), having lasted after the death of Alexander the Great two hundred and ninety-three years. Egypt, reduced to a province, became part of the Roman Empire until the middle of the seventh century A.D., when it was subjugated by the Saracens, or Arabs, the followers of Mahomet.

Sec. 2. THE KINGDOM OF SYRIA UNDER THE SELEUCIDÆ (301–64 B.C.): *Power of Seleucus I.; Antiochus the Great (222–186 B.C.); Intervention of the Romans.*

SELEUCUS I., NICATOR (312–280); FOUNDATION OF ANTIOCH.—Seleucus, surnamed Nicator, or " the Conqueror," had received from the regent Antipater the government of Babylon. Driven from his province by Antigonus, he returned thither in the year 312 and opened the era of the Seleucidæ. Aided by the Babylonians, he extended without difficulty his kingdom to the Indus. Returning from this expedition, he took the title of king (306). The victory of Ipsus gave him possession of Asia to Mount Taurus (301). It was then that, master of Syria, he built on the Orontes the city of Antioch, so named from his father, Antiochus. According to a barbarous custom, he laid the foundation of the new city only after a horrible sacrifice—that of a young girl destined to be the protecting goddess of the new city. Seleucus and his successors fixed their residence at Antioch, which became from that time the capital of the East.

VICTORY OVER LYSIMACHUS (282).—Seleucus had hitherto been allied with Lysimachus, King of Thrace, but towards the close of their lives, when both were more than eighty years old, they became enemies. Lysimachus having murdered the sister of Ptolemy Ceraunus, the latter took refuge at the Syrian court, where Seleucus received him with honor and refused to give him up. Upon this refusal Lysimachus advanced with his army to Cyropedion, in Phrygia, where he was defeated and slain. Seleucus, then surnamed " Conqueror of conquerors," added to his states all of Asia Minor, Thrace, and Macedonia. His empire, omitting Egypt, was as vast as that of Alexander. Exulting in his power and in being the sole survivor of the generals of Alexander, he wished to offer to the gods a solemn sacrifice of thanksgiving, but he was assassinated in the midst of the ceremony by Ptolemy Ceraunus, who caused himself to be proclaimed king of Thrace and Macedon.

ANTIOCHUS I., SOTER (280–260), AND ANTIOCHUS II., THEOS (260–247) ; EMPIRE OF THE PARTHIANS UNDER THE ARSACIDÆ (255).—The fall of the kingdom of Syria began with its

founder's death. Antiochus, his son, surnamed
Soter, or " saviour," because of a slight advantage
he had gained over the Gauls, lost a part of Asia
Minor and left the crown to Antiochus II., who
received the name of Theos, or "god." The
reign of the pretended god was most unhappy.
While engaged in a war against Egypt, the Parthians, provoked by the wickedness of their governor, began to shake off the Syrian yoke and
took for their leader Arsaces, a man of obscure
birth but of great valor and ability. This was
the origin of the Parthian kingdom. The example of successful insurrection set by the Parthians was followed by other neighboring nations,
and the proud monarch of Syria lost all his provinces beyond the Tigris.

* The empire of the Parthians is the most considerable of the
states formed at the expense of the kingdom of Syria. It was the
only power that opposed a determined resistance to the Romans.
The following are the other states of Asia rendered independent in
the third and second centuries B.C. : The kingdom of Persia, detached
from Thrace in 283, was bequeathed to the Romans by Attila III.,
and established as a Roman province in 129. The kingdom of Bithynia was detached from Thrace at the death of Lysander, and made a
Roman province in the year 75. Galatia, given in 278 to the Galatians by the king of Bithynia, became a Roman province in the year
25 B.C. The kingdom of Pontus became independent after the battle
of Ipsus ; its power was greatly increased by Mithridates VI., and it
was attached to the Roman Empire in the year 63. The kingdom of
Cappadocia was attached to the Roman Empire in the year 18 B.C.
Armenia was separated from Syria in 189, and a part of it (Lesser
Armenia) was occupied by the Romans in the year 75 B.C., and the
other part (Greater Armenia) was occupied by the Persians in 428 B.C.
The kingdom of the Jews, detached from the kingdom of Syria by
the Machabees in 167, became a Roman province about six years B.C.

WAR WITH EGYPT; SELEUCUS II., CALLINI-
CUS (247–225), AND SELEUCUS III., CERAUNUS
(225–222).—These reverses obliged Antiochus to
sue for peace of Philadelphus, King of Egypt.
He obtained it on condition that he would repu-
diate Laodice, his wife, and espouse Berenice,
daughter of Philadelphus. This marriage, begun
in crime, led to the most fatal consequences.
Philadelphus dying, Theos renounced Berenice
and took Laodice back. The latter, to prevent
another estrangement, poisoned Theos, got possession of Berenice by stratagem, and cruelly
murdered her and all the Egyptians that followed
her. These crimes did not long remain unpun-
ished. Ptolemy Euergetes avenged the murder
of his sister by putting Laodice to death and the
conquest of a great part of Syria, which he took
from Seleucus Callinicus, son of the cruel queen.
Callinicus, or "the great conqueror," was the
name given in derision to one who allowed himself to be beaten by all his enemies. His son
Ceraunus, or the "Thunderbolt," was not more
worthy of his surname, and was poisoned.

ANTIOCHUS III., THE GREAT (222–186); EX-
PEDITION TO THE EAST; CONQUEST OF JUDEA
(203).—Antiochus III., the second son of Callinicus, ascended the throne when very young, and
merited by his actions the title of Great. At
first his arms were not crowned with success. He
was conquered at Raphia by the Egyptians (217).

But ill-success did not continue. Rid of an ambitious and violent minister who betrayed him, he began to act for himself, and pushed on his enterprises with a vigor that made him indomitable among his neighbors. Having checked the revolt of some leaders who took advantage of his youth to withdraw their allegiance, he led his armies to the East. Here, if he failed to overthrow the empire of the Parthians, he at least stripped it of its late acquisitions and restricted it within the narrow limits of Parthia. Thence Antiochus advanced to the Indus and everywhere established his authority. This expedition lasted seven years, and the prince returned to Antioch with the reputation of a monarch equally prudent and courageous (205).

Antiochus then turned his arms against Judea, which he took with little difficulty from Egypt, then governed by a child. The Jews, ill-content with Egypt, gladly acknowledged allegiance to the kings of Syria.

WAR WITH THE ROMANS; BATTLE OF THERMOPYLÆ (191) AND MAGNESIA (190).—Meanwhile, Antiochus, inflamed by ambition, and animated by his past success, undertook the conquest of Asia Minor. Smyrna and the other Greek cities then enjoyed their liberty and formed so many republics. Seeing themselves unable to cope alone with so formidable an adversary, they sought the protection of the Romans, which was readily given. This politic and ambitious people never refused aid against any power that rivalled theirs. Antiochus was the more emboldened to undertake the war because the famous Hannibal had come to his court. Hannibal had been pursued by the Romans as far as Carthage, and, returning hatred for hatred, he everywhere incited new enemies against the Romans. He represented to the king that the Romans could only be conquered in Italy, and offered himself to conduct the war. Antiochus favored the project, but he either did not know how to profit by it or the Romans left him no time. Wounded and put to flight at Thermopylæ, he returned precipitately into Asia (191). The consul Lucius Scipio closely pursued him and offered him battle near Magnesia, in Lydia. Antiochus accepted and fought with great valor, but the Romans won the day. Antiochus was completely defeated, and, to obtain peace, was obliged to cede to Rome all the provinces of Asia on that side of Mount Taurus and defray all the expenses of the war.

DEATH OF ANTIOCHUS.—When the time came to fulfil his obligation Antiochus found himself in great perplexity. His coffers were empty. In his embarrassment he attempted by night to plunder the rich temple of Persepolis, but was discovered by the inhabitants and killed with all his followers (187). This prince had in general

shown much wisdom and justice, but his conduct during the war with the Romans, and the
shameful peace he was obliged to accept greatly
tarnished his former glory, and his death, caused
by a sacrilegious enterprise, leaves an ineffacable stain on his memory. He had as successor
Seleucus Philopator, his son, whose reign presents nothing remarkable save the criminal and
disastrous attack of Heliodorus, one of his generals, on the Temple of Jerusalem (176).

ANTIOCHUS IV., EPIPHANES (174–164); WAR
IN EGYPT.—Seleucus Philopator was succeeded
by Antiochus, surnamed Epiphanes—that is,
" Illustrious." Scripture more truly styles him
" Contemptible." In fact, he would often leave
his palace and run through the streets of
Antioch. He amused himself by disputing with
artisans about the minutiæ of their trades, and
ridiculously prided himself on knowing more
than they. He would go to parties of pleasure,
and there sing and drink without any regard to
decency. However, he lacked neither courage
nor ambition. He attempted the conquest of
Egypt, and would have achieved it had not the
Romans, who even then spoke as masters to the
most warlike kings, compelled him to desist from
further hostilities (168).

PERSECUTION IN JUDEA (167); THE MACHA
BEES.—Antiochus, enraged at seeing so certain a
conquest snatched from him, discharged his an-

ger on the Jews, and began a cruel persecution
which only the victories of the Machabees could
stop. While his generals were beaten in Judea
he himself was defeated in Persia, and on his return he was struck by the hand of God with a
frightful malady. His flesh fell from him in
pieces or was eaten by swarms of worms, and
the stench became intolerable to his army. It
was from this frightful disease that Antiochus
ended his life (164), and this was, not unjustly,
deemed a divine punishment for the evils he had
inflicted on the people of God.

ANTIOCHUS VIII., GRYPUS (123–97), AND
CLEOPATRA; SYRIA BECOMES A ROMAN PRO-
VINCE (65).—After many troubles and revolutions, occasioned by the ambition of various pretenders, the crown fell into the hands of Antiochus Grypus, so named from the size of his
nose. Cleopatra, his mother, attempted to govern in his name; but when she saw him disposed to govern by himself, that detestable woman,
who had already murdered her two husbands and
one of her sons, attempted to murder Antiochus
also. She prepared a poisoned drink and presented it to him when he returned heated from
exercise. Antiochus, aware of her design, polite-
ly urged her to drink herself. Upon her con-
stant refusal he told her that the only means of
delivering herself from suspicion would be to
drink the draught she had offered him. Cleopa-

tra, seeing no other resource, took the cup. The
poison took effect and delivered Syria from a
monster who, by her crimes, had long been the
plague of the state (120). After the death of
Grypus Syria was torn by wars of rival factions
contending for the sovereignty., Weary of pillage and bloodshed, she declared allegiance to
Tigranes, King of Armenia ; but that prince was
obliged to abandon her to preserve his own
states, and Pompey reduced her to a Roman
province in the year 65 B.C., two hundred and
thirty-seven years after the foundation of the
empire by Seleucus Nicator.

Sec. 3. **KINGDOM OF MACEDONIA** (319–148
B.C.) **AND GREECE** (301–146 B.C.): *Triumph
of the Family of Antigonus in Macedonia ;
Anarchy in Greece ; Reform in Sparta ; Intervention of the Romans ; Kings Philip* (221–
178 B.C.) *and Perseus* (178–168 B.C.); *the
Achæan League ; Aratus and Philopœmen.*

CASSANDER (319–298); END OF THE FAMILY
OF ALEXANDER (294).—Cassander, who occupied Macedonia at the death of his father, Anti-
pator, took the title of king in 306 and entered
the league formed against Antigonus. The victory of Ipsus assured him the peaceful possession
of his kingdom. After his death two children
which he had by Thessalonica, the sister of Al-

exander the Great, disputed for the crown, and the result of their struggle was to lose at the same time both crown and life. With them finished the posterity of Philip and Alexander. Thus these two princes, who had desolated so many provinces and destroyed so many royal families, by a just retribution found in their own house the same evils they had inflicted on so many others. Philip, Alexander, his wives, and all their descendants met violent deaths.

DEMETRIUS I., POLIORCETES (294–286).—One of the sons of Cassander, to secure success against his brother, called to his aid Demetrius Poliorcetes, son of Antigonus, who, after the battle of Ipsus, held several cities in Greece. The ambitious Demetrius, instead of giving aid to the young prince, murdered him, deposed his brother, and caused himself to be acknowledged king of Macedonia (294). When he deemed his throne sufficiently safe, he gave himself up to projects of conquest, and, in fact, contemplated the recovery of all that his father had possessed in Asia. But all at once his army, gained over by the celebrated Pyrrhus, King of Epirus, revolted and refused to follow him. In despair he embarked with a handful of followers and set sail for Asia, resolved to establish himself there or perish. He did neither. After many useless attempts, wandering in the desert and nearly dying of famine, he was obliged to surrender himself to Seleucus Nicator, King of Syria. The latter treated his prisoner with generosity, but the unfortunate prince was attacked with a malady occasioned by inaction, good cheer, and excessive drinking, and died after three years of captivity (283).

ANTIGONUS GONATAS (286–242) ; HIS FILIAL PIETY AND HIS TRIUMPH.—Antigonus, son of Demetrius, and surnamed Gonatas because born at Gona in Thessaly, showed for his father a devotion that has but few parallels in antiquity. On hearing of his captivity he was filled with intense grief. He wrote to all the kings, even to Seleucus himself, begging him to release Demetrius, offering himself as a hostage, and proposing for his ransom to despoil himself of all that he possessed. This heroism of filial love did not escape Him before whom even pagan virtues find their reward. Antigonus Gonatas, by unforeseen circumstances, found himself ere long the king of Macedonia.

Pyrrhus, master of Macedonia (286), was dethroned by Lysimachus, the latter by Seleucus I. (282), and Seleucus himself was assassinated by Ptolemy Ceraunus (280). The same year Ceraunus fell in a battle against the Gauls, who had pillaged the temple of Delphi. Taking advantage of these troubles, Antigonus succeeded in conquering Macedonia (278). It was at first necessary to struggle against his competitor, the

invincible Pyrrhus, King of Epirus, then (274)
employed in a most disastrous expedition in the
south of Italy; but he perished in Argos by the
hand of an old woman, who threw a tile on his
head (272). From that time Antigonus reigned
peacefully in Macedonia; he occupied even a
part of Greece, and became one of the most powerful princes of his age. At a ripe old age he
left the throne to his family, and under them
Macedonia formed an independent kingdom.

SITUATION OF GREECE; REFORM AT SPARTA.
—Greece, from the time of Alexander the Great,
was attached to Macedonia. Two leagues had
been formed there, the one called *Ætolian*, between the cities of Ætolia, and the other called
Achæan, between several cities of Achaia. The
first was but a vain effort to debar Demetrius II.
(242–232), son of Antigonus, who had seized
Bœotia, from Central Greece. The second called
the Macedonians in Peloponnesus against the
city of Sparta. Sparta was well-nigh stripped of
her ancient power. In contempt of the laws of
Lycurgus, riches had been accumulated, and
with them came avarice, luxury, effeminacy, and
voluptuousness, which, in depriving them of their
virtues, deprived them of their glory and prosperity. In the beginning of the reign of Demetrius II., Agis, one of the two kings of Sparta,
conceived the project of reforming his country
and of introducing the laws of Lycurgus. But

———✦———

he fell a victim to his noble design, and the fruit of his zeal was a cruel death inflicted by his fellow-citizens (240).

Cleomenes, brother-in-law of Agis, succeeded him, and was not dismayed by the unhappy fate of his predecessor. He prosecuted his enterprise with vigor. He banished first those who did not second his views; then, convening an assembly, he represented to the Lacedæmonians that he had no interest but that of the republic in renewing among them the institutions of the wise Lycurgus, to whom Sparta in happier times owed all her reputation. Having spoken thus, he was the first to give up all his goods, which were considerable, for the public welfare. His example persuaded more than his words; every one gloried in imitating him. The vices which dishonored Sparta were banished, and the temperance, love of country, and simple habits of the ancient Spartans were revived.

The war that Cleomenes undertook against the Achæans blasted the fruit of his endeavors, and ruined himself (228). The Achæans, pressed by the young prince and unable to resist him, called to their aid the king of Macedonia.

ANTIGONUS DOSON (232–221); BATTLE OF SELLASIA (222).—Demetrius II., dying, had left to his nephew Antigonus the care of his son Philip, yet a child; but Antigonus, exchanging the title of tutor for king, seized the throne and

—✠—

occupied it for twelve years, during which time he merited the surname of Doson—that is, "the Promiser"—as he was always promising and never doing. Seizing this occasion of entering the Peloponnesus, he hastened to the succor of the Achæan league. His arrival did not at first check the progress of Cleomenes, who executed many glorious undertakings. At last Antigonus, having augmented the number of his troops, marched towards Laconia and met Cleomenes stationed in the defile of Sellasia. The battle was obstinately fought. Finally the troops of Antigonus, advancing with levelled lances, forced the enemy from their intrenchments. Cleomenes returned to Sparta and advised the people to receive Antigonus. As for himself, he would neither eat nor drink, but embarked for Egypt, where he was thrown in prison until his death, by order of Ptolemy Philopator. Antigonus entered Sparta not as an enemy but as a friend. He magnanimously gave liberty to Sparta, and returned to Macedonia.

PHILIP (221–178); BATTLE OF CYNOCEPHALÆ (197).—At the death of Antigonus Doson the crown fell to his cousin Philip, son of Demetrius II. This prince had shown while young great prudence, activity, courage, and moderation, and conducted himself according to the precepts of the most virtuous and most experienced in the kingdom. He had also been successful in the war which he undertook with the Achæans against the Etolian league. But his after-life resembled little its good beginning. Prosperity made him proud and haughty, and then he listened to the flatterers who advised him to league with Hannibal and the Carthaginians against the Romans (216). The latter seemed at first to disregard the hostile intentions of Philip ; but, once delivered from Carthage, they sought vengeance. Quintus Flaminius, their general, at the head of a vast army, went to Macedonia in search of Philip. The two armies were separated by the heights of Cynocephalæ. Philip sent a detachment to seize them ; Quintus did likewise. The two detachments, having met, came to blows. They were reinforced and the combat became general. Philip, conquered, was obliged to sue for peace, and to obtain it was compelled to surrender all his vessels, to give his son Demetrius as a hostage, and to evacuate all the cities of Greece which he had seized before the war (197).

THE LIBERTY OF THE GREEKS IS PROCLAIMED (196).—The Isthmian games approached. Quintus returned and found waiting an innumerable concourse of people desirous of hearing the proclamation which was to decide the fate of Greece, for the conditions of peace were not yet known. At last a herald arose and proclaimed in a loud voice that the Senate and Roman people restored to the Greeks liberty and their own laws. These words were received with loud cries of rejoicing. In thus generously according to the Greeks liberty to live according to their own laws Rome also served her own policy, since by so doing she raised a barrier against the power and pretensions of the Macedonian kings; she presented the people yet under their control a bait which they seized with avidity; she divided Greece into as many portions as there were colonies; she left within each of the freed cities all the agitations of a popular government, and without, a thousand springs of jealousy and mutual hatred, which sooner or later would arm them against one another, and end by surrendering them all to the discretion of the Roman people. But the Greeks did not perceive the snare laid for them, and their natural frivolity blinded them in regard to the consequences of their so-called independence till too late.*

DEMETRIUS IS PERSECUTED BY PERSEUS.—Philip cherished a secret animosity against the Romans, and, though he concealed it for some time, could hardly repress it when his affairs gave him some respite and greater hope of success.

---

*In the year 191 the Etolian league, who reproached the Romans for not having recompensed them for their aid in the war against Philip, called into Greece King Antiochus But they, being deserted by the other Greeks, could furnish but little aid to the king of Syria, who was defeated by the Romans at Thermopylæ. The league was dissolved and the Etolians subjected to the Roman yoke (189).

---+---

In the interim his son Demetrius, then a hostage at Rome, so won the senators by his good qualities that he was honorably dismissed to the court of his father. These tokens of regard served but to render him odious in the sight of Philip, who regarded the Romans as his greatest enemies. Another unfavorable circumstance was the jealousy of his brother Perseus. The latter desired to reign, and as he saw that the better claim of his brother, supported too by the affection of the Roman people, would be an insuperable barrier to his ambition, he resolved to remove him by intrigue.

He availed himself of the first opportunity to execute his dark design. On a day of great festivity among the Macedonians the army, divided into two bodies under the command of the two brothers, represented a battle, in which the body led by Demetrius obtained a decided advantage. This was keenly resented by Perseus. At night both princes gave a repast to their respective partisans and friends. Whilst joy and mirth reigned among the guests, Perseus sent a spy to hear what might be said at his brother's banquet. The spy happened to be discovered, and was ill-treated outside of the hall by four persons belonging to the party of Demetrius. The young prince, totally unaware of this incident, invited his guests to accompany him to the residence of his brother, in order to show their goo feeling towards him, and to allay his displeasure if he still entertained any. The proposal was readily accepted. The four young men who had ill-treated the spy, fearing for themselves the same kind of reception which they had given him, concealed swords under their garments to repel any attack. Perseus heard of this before the company arrived. He denied them admittance, and the following day accused Demetrius, in the presence of the king, of attempting to deprive him of life.

DEATH OF DEMETRIUS.—Philip appeared deeply afflicted, and bitterly bewailed the unhappy circumstances which obliged him to judge between his own children, and pronounce one guilty of projected murder or the other of a dreadful calumny. Perseus endeavored very artfully to prove the charge he had advanced, but Demetrius easily repelled it, and proved his innocence (182). Seeing, however, that his affection for the Romans rendered him an object of dislike and suspicion at his father's court, he resolved to set out for Italy. But he was betrayed, and, at the solicitation of Perseus, Philip gave him a poisonous drink. The unhappy father too late discovered the innocence of Demetrius, and expired with the bitter regret of having so cruelly treated a guiltless son, and spared and favored one who alone was deserving of the severest punishment.

PERSEUS (178–168) ; BATTLE OF PYDNA (168) ; MACEDONIA A ROMAN PROVINCE (148).—Perseus inherited the animosity and hostile designs of his father against the Romans, and spent the first years of his reign in making preparations for a new contest, using every species of intrigue either to gain allies for himself or to destroy those of Rome. War was at length openly declared. During three years no event of great importance transpired; but in the fourth, Paulus Æmilius, having been named consul, procured a speedy and happy termination to the war. Perseus himself contributed to his misfortunes by his avarice. He had secured, by the promise of a large sum, the assistance of twenty thousand Gauls. When they arrived he refused to pay the stipulated amount, and the Gauls, furious at this breach of faith, laid waste a great part of the country while returning home, and Perseus lost, through his perfidy, a large number of auxiliaries who might have been of great service.

The Romans, having crossed the passes of Mount Olympus, overtook him near Pydna, where he was entirely defeated and fled to Pella, his capital. He would have retreated still further, but falling with his family into the hands of the consul, he was carried to Rome to grace his conqueror's triumph. Thus precipitated from the throne he had mounted by fratricide, he died from excess of grief (167). Macedonia was at first declared free, but her liberty gave birth to troubles which obliged the Romans to reduce her to a province (148). So ended the kingdom of Macedonia, which lasted one hundred and seventy-five years after the death of Alexander the Great.

THE ACHÆAN LEAGUE (280); ARATUS DE- LIVERS CORINTH (244).—The Achæan league, so named from Achaia, a district of Peloponnesus, owed its influence not to its riches or power but to its great reputation for integrity and justice. The perfect order which reigned in this little republic drew to it several neighboring cities. Sicyon set the example, and it was Aratus, one of the principal citizens, who, having delivered his city from the yoke of an usurper, persuaded its inhabitants to join the Achæan league (251).

A few years later, Aratus, chosen general of the Achæans, rendered an important service to all Greece by wresting the Corinthian citadel, which was the key of the Peloponnesus, from the hands of the Macedonians. He executed this perilous enterprise with uncommon disinterestedness and generosity, himself defraying the expenses of the expedition. When everything was ready, he chose four hundred brave soldiers and led them at night to the foot of the Corinthian ramparts. Aratus, with one hundred men, scaled the walls, surprised the guard, and opened an entrance for the others. The resolute band marched towards

the citadel. They met a small guard of four
men who had lights in their hands, and whom
they clearly saw, themselves being unseen in the
darkness. They killed three of the four, but the
other, only wounded, fled and gave the alarm.
In a moment the trumpets sounded, and the
whole city was filled with uproar and confusion.
Still Aratus marched on and began with his
bold followers to climb the craggy rock upon
which the citadel was built. They reached the
height at a spot where the rampart was less difficult of access, but, failing to surprise it, were
obliged to fight the garrison hand to hand.

Meanwhile the three hundred left behind, not
being able to discover the path which Aratus had
followed, drew themselves up in a body beneath
an overhanging rock, and there waited in the
utmost anxiety. They heard the cries of the
combatants, but as the noise was echoed by the
neighboring mountains, they could not distinguish whence it came and knew not which way
to direct their course. Just at that moment a
body of Macedonian soldiers hastened past to the
relief of the citadel. As soon as they had passed
the Achæans fell upon them, and, killing some,
put the rest to flight. A guide then came from
Aratus to conduct them to the citadel, where
their assistance was greatly needed; having at
last joined their friends, they made so vigorous
an assault that the garrison could no longer

resist and the victorious Achæans saw themselves
at break of day masters of the citadel. Aratus
had no sooner secured his conquest than, disre-
garding his fatigue, he descended into the city
and was met in the theatre by a vast concourse
of people. When he appeared all were eager to
testify their profound respect and gratitude by
repeated acclamations. Aratus delivered to the
Corinthians the keys of their city, which had not
been in their hands from the time of King
Philip. This act of generosity won them to his
cause and they entered the Achæan league.

MISTAKES AND DISFAVOR OF ARATUS.—Aratus, during the ensuing year, restored freedom
to several other cities of Peloponnesus, till then
the prey of tyrants. This conduct rendered him
very dear to the Greeks, whose predominant
characteristic was an ardent love of liberty; but
his wars against the Lacedæmonians detracted
much from his reputation. Cleomenes was willing to join the Achæans on condition that he
should be appointed chief leader, but Aratus
was unwilling to resign an honor he had enjoyed
for more than thirty years, and thus lose the reward of his services. This refusal exposed him
to the attacks of the Spartans. Repeatedly defeated and anxious to arrest the course of their
victories, he committed another great mistake,
namely, that of calling to his assistance Antigonus Doson, the King of Macedonia. The latter

defeated Cleomenes, and even dethroned him
(222); but he made the Achæans pay dearly for
his services. He ordered the citadel of Corinth
to be again surrendered to Macedonia, and had
himself named general of the confederacy. The
Achæans thus fell into a sort of subjection to
the kings of Macedonia, until the Macedonians
were defeated by the Romans, and Philopœmen
restored by his victories the glory and power of
the republic.

PHILOPŒMEN; HIS MILITARY TALENTS.—
Philopœmen was born at Megalopolis, a city of
the Achæan republic. From his youth he accustomed himself to a hard, laborious, and active
life, and persistently pursued the practise of such
exercises as might render him a great warrior. At the age of twenty years he signalized
himself in the famous battle of Sellasia, and it
was to him more than any other that Antigonus
was indebted for his victory. The king acknowledged this, after the battle, in a manner very
flattering. Feigning to be angry because the
cavalry had charged before the signal was given,
and being answered by the commander that the
fault was to be laid entirely to the account of a
young Megalopolitan officer, the king replied:
"This young man, by seizing the proper moment
of action, has performed the part of an experienced and prudent general, and you, the general,
have acted the part of an unskilful young man."

—✠—

DEFEAT OF THE TYRANT MACHANIDAS (206).
—Philopœmen for his great services was appointed commander in-chief of the Achæans. This
nation was at that time engaged in a war against
the tyrant of Sparta, Machanidas, who desired
to make conquest of the whole of the Peloponnesus, and had advanced as far as Mantinea.
Philopœmen gave battle near that place. The
beginning of the action was far from being favorable to him; his left wing was completely broken. Philopœmen, undismayed, awaited some
opportunity to retrieve himself, which was soon
offered. Instead of attacking both the front and
the flank of the Achæans, Machanidas wasted
time in pursuit of fugitives. Philopœmen quickly occupied the ground thus abandoned, and not
only separated the tyrant from the main body of
his troops, but cut the latter to pieces. Machanidas at length returned from the pursuit;
but it was too late. At the very instant when
he was spurring his horse to rejoin the remnants
of his army, Philopœmen pierced him with his
spear, and by this bold exploit completed and
secured a victory the fruit in every respect of his
superior talents (206).

**THE TYRANT NABIS; SPARTA JOINS THE
ACHÆAN LEAGUE (191).**—The death of Machanidas did not restore to the Spartans their
ancient liberty. Nabis succeeded him and proved even more tyrannical. He was a monster of

— ✠ —

cruelty and avarice. He invented an automaton which represented his wife. This image had hands, arms, and the breast bristling with sharp iron points concealed under magnificent garments. When he was refused money by any citizen he said: "Perhaps I do not possess the art of persuading; but my wife will be more winning than I." With these words he would conduct his victim to the machine, where he was tortured till he promised to give the desired amount. Nabis having attacked the Achæans, was signally defeated, and, returning to Sparta, fell by the sword. Philopœmen was no sooner informed of this than he hastened to Sparta, where he found everything in confusion. Assembling the chief citizens, he persuaded them, and through them the whole city, to join the Achæan league (191).

DISINTERESTEDNESS OF PHILOPŒMEN; HIS DEATH (183).—The Lacedæmonians resolved to show their gratitude to Philopœmen by presenting to him Nabis's property. But so well known was the integrity of Philopœmen that not one of the Spartans would be the bearer of the present. It became necessary to intrust it to Timolaus, a stranger, to whom Philopœmen was bound by the ties of hospitality. He therefore went to Megalopolis and took lodging with Philopœmen, who gave him a kind reception. Having observed the virtue of this great man, the simplicity of his habits, the nobleness of his sentiments, he dared not say a word of the present he was to offer, and, having given some other pretext for his visit, returned as he came. Nor was he more successful on a second visit. Being sent a third time, he ventured to speak of it.

Philopœmen listened with attention, then immediately went to Sparta, where he advised the people not to bribe with money those who were virtuous, but rather to purchase with it the silence of the wicked, that they might no longer occasion disorders. Such was the disinterestedness of Philopœmen that he was deservedly styled the "last of the Greeks," because after him Greece produced no man worthy of her ancient glory. At the age of seventy years he was made prisoner in an engagement with the Messenians, and was basely and cruelly put to death. The Achæans, in order to avenge the loss of their general, punished with inexorable severity those who had a part in the death of Philopœmen and performed in his honor magnificent obsequies, which resembled a triumph rather than a funeral.

DEFEAT OF THE ACHÆANS AT LEUCOPETRA; GREECE BECOMES A ROMAN PROVINCE.—After the death of Philopœmen the Achæan republic continued for some time the leading state of Greece. Athens and Thebes were no longer of importance. Corinth and Sparta belonged to it.

————✠————

But this prosperity came to an end. Avarice and rashness gave rise to many disturbances, and when the Romans proffered their services to settle the disputes, the Achæans had the imprudence to provoke their resentment. This led to their ruin, they being too weak to battle with success against Rome. The consul Mummius advanced towards Corinth with the Roman legions. The Achæans went to give them battle at Leucopetra. The former placed their wives and children on the neighboring heights to be spectators of the combat; they also brought a large number of vehicles to be loaded with the spoils which they expected to capture from the enemy, so certainly did these infatuated people anticipate success. Never was there more groundless and rash confidence, for in a short time the Achæans were utterly routed.

Diæus, the Achæan general and the chief instigator of the war, fled to Megalopolis, where, having killed his wife and children and set fire to his house, he poisoned himself, a fitting end for one who could plunge his country into such frightful misery. Mummius gave up Corinth to be plundered by his soldiers; they slew every man found in it, and sold the women and children. The whole city was then fired and the walls demolished.*

* The Romans spared only the statues, pictures, and most precious marbles. Their after conduct proves that it was love of riches and

So fell Corinth, the same year as Carthage (146 B.C.) The Achæan league was annihilated, and Mummius destroyed the walls of all the confederated cities, and deprived their inhabitants of all warlike weapons. Greece became a Roman province under the name of Achaia.

CAUSES OF THE SUBJUGATION OF GREECE; HER PERMANENT INFLUENCE.—The chief cause of the subjugation and fall of Greece was the disunion which armed its different states against each other. As long as the Greeks were united they overthrew and repelled all invaders. Victorious against the attacks of the barbarians, they fell a prey to their mutual jealousy. Sparta and Athens especially engaged in long and bloody strifes. The kings of Macedonia availed themselves of these intestine divisions to become masters of Greece. Rome finished what the Macedonians had but begun, and this famous country was at length absorbed in the Roman Empire. Greece, however, preserved a kind of sovereignty of which her conquerors could not deprive her, and to which even they themselves rendered implicit homage. She continued to be the teacher of the sciences and of the fine arts, and the model of refined taste in the productions

---

not of fine arts that prompted this clemency. Some soldiers desiring a chess-board, took for the purpose a master-piece of painting which was afterwards sold at auction to Attila, King of Pergamus, for $3,600. Mummius, supposing that so valuable a painting must have some beauty, hastened to annul the sale and sent the picture to Rome.

of human genius. It was to an assiduous study of the Greek language and literature that Rome owed her Terence, Cicero, Virgil, Livy, and Horace, whose immortal genius shares with that of the Greeks the admiration of posterity.

CONCLUSION.—In reviewing the great events that decide the fortunes of nations, as of individuals, we cannot fail to recognize the hand of Providence. The Egyptians are subjugated by the Assyrians, the latter by the Persians, the Persians by the Greeks, and lastly the Greek empire, like the other powers of the earth, is lost in that empire whose boundaries were nearly co-extensive with the then known world. This union of almost all nations under one head seems to fulfil the prediction that the Greek and Latin languages would form the basis of all languages. In short, when Rome rests from her conquests the Son of Man appears to establish a new empire, which is the beginning and end of all others, which falls not in the ruin of others, and to which alone eternity is promised.

Feb. 13th

REVIEW QUESTIONS.

EGYPT.

Who founded the dynasty of the Lagi? What was his character? In what did he place the true greatness of kings? By whom was he succeeded? Describe the light-house of Pharos. What additions did Ptolemy II. make to the Alexandrian library? What was his chief care ? What did he make Alexandria ? How were its inhabitants divided ? Why did Ptolemy III. invade Syria ? What did he accomplish ? By whom was Ptolemy IV. attacked ? Describe the battle of Raphia. How did his success affect Ptolemy IV.? Who was his successor ? By what only is he known ? Against whom did his son wage war ? How was the march of Antiochus checked ? How did Popilius act ? What did the Ptolemies after Antiochus withdrew from Egypt ? What was the result ? What can you say of Physeon ? By whom was Ptolemy XI. protected ? Why was he obliged to fly from Egypt ? Relate an incident of his reign ? To whom did Ptolemy XII. leave his crown ? Why did they disagree ? What can you say of Pompey ? How did Cleopatra regain the throne ? What can you say of Ptolemy XIII. Of Mark Antony ? Of Cleopatra's death ? How long did the kingdom of Egypt last ? How long did it continue a part of the Roman Empire ?

SYRIA.

What can you say of Seleucus Nicator ? Of the city of Antioch ? What was the cause of the war between Seleucus and Lysimachus ? Its result ? What of the ingratitude of Ptolemy Ceraunus ? By whom was Seleucus succeeded ? What can you say of him ? When did the Parthians shake off the Syrian yoke ? On what terms was peace granted by Egypt ? The consequences thereof ? What was the character of Antiochus III. ? How far did his authority extend ? How long did his expedition last ? By whom was he gladly received ? What causes led to his war with the Romans ? In what two battles was Antiochus defeated ? What terms were imposed upon him by the Romans ? Describe his death. How was his early glory tarnished ? By whom was he succeeded ? What of him ? What was the character of Antiochus Epiphanes ? By whom was he compelled to retire from Egypt ? On whom did he turn his arms ? Describe his death. What can you say of Antiochus Grypus ? Of his mother Cleopatra ? How did he escape the poisoned cup ? What befell Syria after his death ? What other Asiatic kingdoms became Roman provinces in the third and second centuries B.C. ?

MACEDONIA.

What followed the death of Cassander ? What can you say of Philip and Alexander ? Who now seized the throne of Macedonia ? Why did his army desert him ? To whom was he obliged to surrender ? How was he treated ? Describe the filial piety of Antigonus Gonatas ? How was it rewarded ? Who was his most formidable opponent ? How and where did Pyrrhus end his life ? What of Antigonus after the death of Pyrrhus ? What was the origin of the

Etolian league? The Achæan league? What was the condition of Sparta at this time? Who endeavored to restore her former glory? His reward? What course did Cleomenes pursue? Against whom did he wage war? Whom did they call to their aid? What can you say of Antigonus Doson? Describe the battle of Sellasia. What became of Cleomenes? Who succeeded Antigonus Doson? His character when young? In after life? How did he incur the hostility of the Romans? Who marched against him? Where did the hostile forces meet? What terms was Philip obliged to accept? Relate the manner in which the independence of Greece was proclaimed? Was this liberty really beneficial to Greece? By what was the end of Philip's life embittered? Describe the plot of Perseus. Its failure. What followed? Describe the unhappy position of Philip. What became of Demetrius? How did Perseus spend the first years of his reign? By whom was he defeated? How did he aid in bringing about this result? What of Perseus after the battle of Pydna? In what year B.C., and how many years after the death of Alexander, did Macedonia become a Roman province?

THE ACHÆAN LEAGUE.

To what did the Achæan league owe its influence? Describe the capture of the citadel of Corinth. How did Aratus tarnish his reputation? How did the Macedonians again obtain possession of the citadel? Who was Philopœmen? What can you say of his character? Of his conduct at the battle of Sellasia? How did the king recognize his bravery? Between whom was the battle of Mantinea fought? Describe it. How did Philopœmen secure a complete victory? Who succeeded Machanidas? What was his character? What followed his defeat and death? Illustrate the noble disinterestedness of Philopœmen. What was he deservedly styled? Describe his death. How was it avenged? How did the Achæan league terminate? Describe the battle of Leucopetra. What became of Diæus? What befell the city of Corinth? In what year and under what name did Greece become a Roman province? Describe the chief causes which led to the fall of Greece. In what manner, however, did she still maintain her supremacy? What conclusion must be drawn from the great events hereinbefore described? What grand and enduring result do all these mighty revolutions clearly indicate?

CHRONOLOGICAL TABLE

OF

ANCIENT HISTORY.

From the Dispersion of Men to B.C. 2000.

Foundation of Babylon and Ninive; the Chanaanites in the Land of Chanaan; the Phœnicians invent navigation; Misraim in Egypt; Foundation of Memphis; Construction of the great Pyramids; Lake Mœris; Foundation of Thebes; the Labyrinth; Invasion of the Hyksos; the Pelasgians in Greece and Italy.

From B.C. 2000 to 1600.

Vocation of Abraham, 1921; Sway of the Chaldeans; Joseph in Egypt; Expulsion of the Hyksos, about 1700; Thoutmosis I. and III.; Conquests in Asia; the Hellenes in Greece, about 1600.

From B.C. 1600 to 1300.

Ramses II., or Sesostris; the Hebrews leave Egypt; Josue makes the Conquest of the Land of Chanaan; twentieth Egyptian Dynasty, about 1311; Foundation of the first Assyrian Empire, 1814.

From B.C. 1300 to 1000.

The Heroic Age of Greece; Expedition of the Argonauts about 1226; Wars of the Seven Chiefs and of the Epi-

gones ; the Philistines destroy Sidon, 1209 ; Taking
of Troy, 1184 ; Usurpation of the twentieth Egyptian
Dynasty by the High-Priest of Ammon ; end of the
Egyptian Sway in Asia ; Conquests of Tiglath-Pileser I. about 1100 ; return of the Heraclidæ, or Invasion of the Dorians in Peloponnesus, 1104 ; Saul King,
1095–1054 ; David, 1054–1015 ; Death of Codrus
1045 ; Appointment of Archons of Athens ; Solomon
1015–976 ; Dedication of Solomon's Temple.

From B.C. 1000 to 800.

Schism of the Ten Tribes, 976 ; War of Sesac against Ro-
boam, 971 ; Zenith of the first Assyrian Empire under
Sardanapalus III. and Salmanasar IV. ; Legislation of
Lycurgus, about 885 ; Foundation of Carthage, 872 ;
Jonas at Ninive, about 825.

From B.C. 800 to 700.

End of the first Assyrian Empire, 789 ; Phul imposes tri-
bute on the Kingdom of Israel ; the first Olympiad,
776 ; Foundation of Rome, 753 ; Nabonassar, 747 ;
Foundation of the second Assyrian Empire, 744 ;
First Messenian War, 744–724 ; Ethiopian Kings in
Egypt, 725 ; Taking of Samaria and Destruction of the
Kingdom of Israel, 718 ; Dejoces, King of the Medes,
710 ; War of Sennacherib against Ezechias, King of
Juda.

From B.C. 700 to 600.

Second Messenian War, 684 ; Combat of the Horatii and
the Curiatii, 667 ; the Twelve Kings of Egypt, 665
Psammeticus, 650 ; Zenith of the second Assyrian
Empire under Assar-Haddon and Sardanapalus VI. ;
Defeat and Death of Phraortes, 635 ; Destruction of
Ninive, 625 ; Laws of Draco, 624   Accession of Ta'-

—✦—

.quin the Elder ; Battle of Mageddo, 610 ; Battle of Circesium, 604.

From B.C. 600 to 500.

Foundation of Marseilles, 600 ; Battle of the Eclipse, 595 ; Laws of Solon, 593 ; End of the Kingdom of Juda, 587 ; Taking of Tyre by Nabuchodonosor, 574 ; Usurpation of Pisistratus at Athens, 561 ; Victory of Cyrus over the Babylonians, 555 ; Battle of Thymbra, 544 ; Taking of Babylon by Cyrus, 538 ; Edict in favor of the Jews, 536 ; Conquest of Egypt by Cambyses, 525 ; Accession of Darius I., son of Hystaspes, 521 ; Taking of Babylon, 518 ; The sons of Pisistratus driven from Athens, 510, and the Tarquins from Rome 509 ; Disastrous Expedition of Darius I. against the Scythians ; Revolt of Ionia.

From B.C. 500 to 400.

Burning of Sardis, 500 ; Institution of the Dictatorship at Rome, 498 ; Withdrawal of the Plebeians to Mons Sacer, 493 ; Expedition of Mardonius, 492 ; Battle of Marathon, 490 ; Leonidas at Thermopylæ ; Battles of Himera and Salamis, 480 ; Battles of Platæa and Mycale, 479 ; Victory of Cimon at the mouth of the Eurymedon, 470 ; Death of Themistocles, 466 ; Third Messenian War, 464 ; Edict of Artaxerxes Longimanus for the Rebuilding of the Walls of Jerusalem, 454; the Decemvirs at Rome, 450 ; End of the Median Wars, 449 ; Institution of Military Tribunes at Rome, 444 ; Peloponnesian War, 431 ; Plague at Athens, Death of Pericles, 428 ; Expedition of the Athenians into Sicily, 415 ; Battle of the Arginusæ Islands, 406 ; Battle of Ægos-Potamus, 405 ; Taking of Athens, 404 ; Thrasybulus delivers Athens from the Thirty Tyrants, 403 ; Battle of Cunaxa, 401 ; Retreat of the Ten Thousand, 401–400.

—✛—

From B.C. 400 to 300.

Death of Socrates, 400 ; Expedition of Agesilaüs into Asia, 397–395 ; Repulse of Himilco before Syracuse, 396 ; Victory of Agesilaüs at Coronea, and of Conon on the Cnidus, 394 ; Taking of Rome by the Gauls, 390 ; Treaty of Antalcidas, 387 ; Liberation of Thebes, 378 ; Battles of Leuctra, 371, and Mantinea, 363 ; Accession of Philip, 360 ; Birth of Alexander, 356 ; Sacred War against the Phocians, 355 ; Success of Timoleon in Sicily, 345–343 ; Battle of Chæronea, 338 ; Accession of Alexander the Great, 336 ; Destruction of Thebes, 335 ; Battles of Granicus, 334, Issus, 333, and Arbela, 331 ; the Caudine Forks, 331 ; Death of Darius, 330 ; Death of Alexander, 323 ; Lamian War, 322 ; Death of Phocion, 317 ; Era of the Seleucidæ, 312 ; Expedition of Agathocles into Africa, 311–307 ; the Five Kings, 306 ; Siege of Rhodes, 304–303 ; Battle of Ipsus, 301.

From B.C. 300 to 200.

Foundation of Antioch, 299 ; Death of Cassander, 298 ; Demetrius Poliorcetes, King of Macedon, 294 ; the Romans subdue the Samnites, 290 ; Pyrrhus, King of Epirus, seizes Macedon, 286 ; Defeat and Death of Lysimachus, 282 ; Death of Seleucus I. and Ptolemy Ceraunus, 280 ; Pillage of the Temple of Delphi by the Gauls, 279 ; the Galatians in Asia Minor, 278 ; the Version of the Septuagint, 275 ; Pyrrhus defeated by the Romans at Beneventum, 275 ; Death of Philip at Argos, 272 ; Beginning of the Punic Wars, 264 ; Regulus in Africa, 256 ; Foundation of the Empire of the Parthians under the Arsacidæ, 255 ; Aratus frees Corinth, 244 ; Battle of Sellasia, 222 ; Philip, King of Macedon, 221 ; Hannibal gains the Victories of Ticinus and Trebia, 218, and Cannæ, 216 ; Victory

of Philopœmen at Mantinea, 206 ; Victory of Scipio
at Zama, 202.

From B.C. 200 to 100.

Battle of Cynocephalæ, 197 ; the Freedom of the Greeks
proclaimed, 196 ; Defeat of Antiochus at Thermopylæ,
191, and at Magnesia, 190 ; Death of Philopœmen,
183 ; Battle of Pydna, 168 ; the Circle of Popilius ;
Persecution of Antiochus, 170 ; the Machabees, 167 ;
Submission of Gallia Cisalpina, 163 ; Destruction of
Corinth and Carthage, 146 ; Destruction of Numantia,
133 ; Jugurtha delivered to the Romans, 106 ; Victories of Marius over the Teutons at Aix, 102, and over
the Cimbri at Vercelli, 101.

From B.C. 100 to Birth of Jesus Christ.

Death of Marius, 86 ; Dictatorship of Sylla, 82 ; Bithynia
made a Roman Province, 75, as also Syria, 64 ; Death
of Mithridates the Great, 68 ; Accession of Cleopatra,
52 ; Conquest of Gaul by Cæsar, 58–50 ; Battle of
Pharsalia, 48 ; Herod usurps the Throne of Judea, 40 ;
Death of Cleopatra, 80 ; Cappadocia becomes a Roman
Province, 18 ; the Emperor Augustus closes the Temple of Janus ; BIRTH OF OUR LORD JESUS CHRIST.

A TABLE OF PROPER NAMES

Used in this book, showing on which syllable the emphasis should be placed.

Æ'olus.
Æs'chines.
Æs'chylus.
Agath'ocles.
Agesila'us.
Ag'idæ.
Alcibi'ades.
Alcmæ'on.
Alcmæo'nidæ.
Ama'sis.
Ameno'phis.
Amo'sis.
Anaxag'oras.
Antig'onus.
Anti'ochus.
Antip'ater.
Apollodo'rus.
A'pries.
Arbe'la.
Archida'mus.
Areop'agus.
Aristi'des.
Aristode'mus.
Aristogi'ton.
Aristom'enes.

Arsac'idæ.
Artapher'nes.
Asty'ages.
Aule'tes.
Autoch'thones.

Bel'esis.
Bel'ochus.
Bœo'tia.
Bry'gi.

Callic'rates.
Callicrat'idas.
Camby'ses.
Chalce'don.
Chaldæ'a.
Cham.
Charila'us.
Chi'lo.
Ci'mon.
Cleobu'lus.
Cleom'brotus.
Cleom'enes.
Clis'thenes.
Crœ'sus.

Cyax'ares.

Cynoceph'alæ.

Cyrena'ica.

Cyre'ne.

Cyropedi'on.

Dari'us.

Da'tis.

Dej'oces.*

Diodo'rus.

Diog'enes.

Elate'a.

Epaminon'das.

Eph'ori.

Epiph'anes.

Epi'rus.

Ete'ocles.

Euer'getes.

Eu'menes.

Euphra'tes.

Eurip'ides.

Euripon'tidæ.

Eurym'edon.

Eurys'thenes.

Grani'cus.

Gylip'pus.

Heracli'dæ.

Him'era.

Hippar'chus.

Hippoc'rates.

Hyk'sos.

Idume'a.

Itho'mus.

Laod'ice.

Leucop'etra.

Longi'nus.

Lysan'der.

Lysim'achus.

Machan'idas.

Mantine'a.

Megaby'zus.

Messe'ne.

Mile'tus.

Milti'ades.

Mityle'ne.

Myc'ale.

Myce'næ.

Nabo'polasar.

Ne'cho.

Nica'tor.

Nic'ias.

* Also spelled Del'oces.

Œd'ipus.
Œ'ta.

Peloponne'sus.
Per'icles.
Phal'aris.
Philome'tor.
Philop'ator.
Philopœ'men.
Pisis'tratus.
Pit'tacus.
Platæ'a.
Poliorce'tes.
Potidæ'a.
Procli'dæ.
Pythag'oras.

Raph'ia.

Sal'amis.

Salmana'sar.
Sardanapa'lus.
Sennache'rib.
Suffe'tes.

Tage'tus.
Tan'ais.
Tha'les.
The'bes.
Themis'tocles.
Thermop'ylæ.
Thoutmo'sis.
Thucyd'ides.
Timo'leon.
Tisam'enes.

Xen'ophon.
Xerx'es.

Zop'yrus.